EBURY PRESS

ANCIENT CHANTS FOR MODERN LIVING

A published author of three books, Aatmanika Ram is a wife, mother and dog mom. A self-proclaimed eco-warrior, food developer and interior decorator, she practises circular economy in more ways than one.

Aatmanika has a master's in nutrition and has worked in project management in several organizations such as IBM. She has to her credit several years of experience, not just as an author, but also as an expatriate who has travelled and lived in many countries including India, Canada, Thailand, the United Arab Emirates, the United Kingdom and France. The exposure to varied cultures, her strong family-centred values and innate curiosity drove her to explore and write about her life experiences in *Shells on the Beach* (2012), an anthology, and her artistic taste and the desire to bring out the essence of good human values found expression in the poetic fiction, *The Rose Petal Trail: A Sutra for Timeless Love* (2012).

Aatmanika continues to learn to master the fine art of striking a balance between being authentic and adapting oneself to change (the only constant in life). She can be reached at aatmanika.blogs@gmail.com.

PRAISE FOR THE BOOK

'*Ancient Chants for Modern Living* is full of gems for both the young and old. It is a known fact that chanting shlokas brings a lot of peace to the mind and body. The author's attempt to harness the benefits of chanting shlokas to help overcome day-to-day problems affecting the modern world is to be commended. The Shankar Mahadevan Academy (http:// www.shankarmahadevanacademy.com/learn-devotionalmusic/) helps you develop the admirable spiritual discipline of daily shloka chanting with the help of its online devotional courses. I am very happy to see that a book has been written to understand how and where to use the shlokas in this modern-day world. I sincerely hope this book benefits those who are willing to make a change to their lives'

—Shankar Mahadevan, award-winning composer and singer

'All of us are aware that dietary information is flooding every type of media these days. Unfortunately, a lot of it is borrowed matter from the West. The ancient wisdom of our great country had been sidelined for all these centuries. I am very happy and proud to learn that Aatmanika Ram has come out with a book that combines recommendations for a balanced diet with healing yoga practices and chanting of shlokas to overcome physical problems. *Ancient Chants for Modern Living* is a much-needed book in today's world'

—Malathi Mohan, former president of the Indian Dietetic Association

'Aatmanika Ram, in her book *Ancient Chants for Modern Living*, strives to bridge the distance between modern-day lives and our rich cultural heritage in a wonderful way. As a historian of temples and temple architecture, I find that the effort that Aatmanika has taken would be very appealing to both those who lead modern-day, fast-paced lives as well as those who are very deeply connected even now to our rich cultural heritage. The temples that are spoken of in the book hold very deep treasures and are a must-visit, to feel connected to our rich heritage. Temples in India not only provide positive vibes to the mind and body but also have a rich history behind them. As with anything, understanding the history and deeper meaning behind them is sure to make the journey of learning more enjoyable'

—Dr Chithra Madhavan, research scholar in ancient history and archaeology

'The importance of yoga in today's world cannot be stressed enough. Shlokas play a very important role in these sadhanas and help us connect with the Almighty and [find] peace within ourselves. Practising yoga alone cannot solve physical issues. The association of shloka chanting, a balanced diet, good yogic practice and the correct attitude have been brought out very well in Aatmanika's book, *Ancient Chants for Modern Living*'

—Dr Ranjan Kumar Panda, yoga instructor, Dubai

ANCIENT CHANTS

FOR MODERN LIVING

AATMANIKA RAM

EBURY PRESS

An imprint of Penguin Random House

EBURY PRESS

Ebury Press is an imprint of the Penguin Random House group of companies whose addresses can be found at global.penguinrandomhouse.com

Published by Penguin Random House India Pvt. Ltd
4th Floor, Capital Tower 1, MG Road,
Gurugram 122 002, Haryana, India

Penguin
Random House
India

First published by Westland Ltd 2016
Published in Ebury Press by Penguin Random House India 2024

10 9 8 7 6 5 4 3 2 1

ISBN 9780143459736

Typeset by PrePSol Enterprises Pvt. Ltd.
Printed at Replika Press Pvt. Ltd, India

www.penguin.co.in

MIX
Paper from
responsible sources
FSC® C016779

Contents

Acknowledgements

I am compiling this book based on my interactions and interviews with renowned people in the profession, such as Shrimati Subashini, my mother, who used to be the editor in charge of *Gnanabhoomi*, a Hindu religious magazine. She has visited over five hundred temples all over India and has had the honour of writing about temple history and the greatness of these religious places in the magazine. She has interviewed various saints and gurus every month for fifteen years to understand the nuances of Sanathana Dharma. She has also written research articles on temples under the pen name of Sabari for Gnanabhoomi. Her writings and knowledge of Hindu religion and practices is voluminous. I was fortunate to travel with her to most of the temples that she visited. Thank you Smt. Subashini, my first guru. I take your blessings and hope that you will be a guiding light for generations to come. Your immense faith in the Almighty will be an inspiration forever.

(Late) Professor M.V. Hariharan and Smt. Malathi Hariharan gave me immense support in editing this book. Their knowledge of Sanskrit and shlokhas ensured the correct choice of shlokha for every challenge that modern life throws at us. Professor M.V. Hariharan was a professor from the prestigious IIT (Mumbai) and also my dear father-in-law. His wife, my mother-in-law, the reason behind his success, now spends her retired life in Chennai.

A big thanks to Deepthi Talwar, Varun Sudarshan and the publishers. Truly appreciate the inputs given for this book.

My gratitude to my husband and my daughter, for being my perennial sounding board and for encouraging me in this journey of book publishing.

The inputs you all have provided have added immense value to this book. Thank you all for being a part of my life and elevating my level and understanding of shlokas and chants.

Introduction

If you have never been on a rollercoaster, then you should try it out. Now. It's an absolutely exhilarating experience. First, the long serpentine queue for the ride. Once you're through the entrance and on the rollercoaster, you're taken up almost torturously right to the precipice. Then there is the drop. You start falling. You feel yourself plummeting feet first into open space, your head following in free fall. The blood rushes to your head and you are filled with fear and excitement. Finally, at the end of the ride, you feel a sense of the joy at having faced this challenge. It's all over before you even know it. You look around and see thrilled expressions everywhere. You're filled with a sense of belonging, of having shared an extreme experience together. Or maybe you're just confused about how anybody could enjoy something like this.

When you're on the ride, you have only two choices: you can either scream with fear or you can enjoy the ride.

Our journey in this Universe is the same. You can either enjoy the ride or live in absolute fear throughout your life. Your choice.

But why should life always be about making choices? Why does it seem like we are always at a crossroads — one wrong move and everything comes crashing down like a pack of cards? How do we make informed choices all the time? How can we live fearlessly with so much uncertainty and choice? I guess there is no simple answer to these profound questions that go through every person's mind from generation to generation, irrespective of where they live or which culture they belong to.

It is every parent's dream to ensure their child is well equipped before they can fly away from their nest. Providing for the education, health and safety of the child is what every parent does with love and dedication. But do we really equip the child for the real world? Providing for physical comforts does not assure a smooth ride. Are we preparing the child to be able to face emotional upheavals and mental challenges in life, especially if she / he has had a very protective upbringing?

How do we ensure that the child can be strong and empowered in every challenging situation?

The parental instinct is to protect the child from every kind of harm. Some psychologists like to call this 'overprotective' or 'smothering the child'. But there's a two-fold reason parents do this. First, they unconditionally love the child. Second, they want to do all it takes to ensure that the child doesn't get into a bad situation. This latter reason is not parental instinct but sheer survival — why fire-fight a problem when it can be prevented instead?

The bottom line is that everybody wants not just a grand finale for their lives but also a great beginning and memorable chapters in the middle.

Is that possible? Well, the answers to all these open-ended questions lie in your hands.

I have experienced great joy in compiling this information and presenting it to you. The intention was not to fill your minds with information and make you feel overwhelmed, but to show you that there is always a light during dark times. Chanting and believing in the Almighty merely allows us to see where that light is, and choose the right path.

A disclaimer: These remedial actions have worked wonders for me and people known to me. To follow the yoga asanas, please ensure you are physically fit. Consult with your physician before you proceed.

The devotional songs that are mentioned in this book are those I have on my own playlists. They have helped me through all the challenges that I've faced. I have mentioned specific singers to help the reader download the original and legal version of the song with ease. The inclusion of the songs is purely a personal choice and is not influenced by any marketing strategy. I have found peace listening to them, and wish the same for all my readers.

I would like to take the opportunity to ask for forgiveness from the Almighty for any mistakes made unknowingly in this book:

Oṃ kṣamābhārtre namaḥ (I bow to Lord Ganesha who is the chief deity of forgiveness).

From my soul to yours
Aatmanika

Pronunciation Guide for the Shlokas in this Book

International Alphabet of Sanskrit Transliteration (IAST)

The shlokas in this book are all transliterated from the Devanagari script into English. This transliteration is based on the International Alphabet of Sanskrit Transliteration (IAST). IAST is the most popular transliteration scheme and is used in printed publications.

The transliteration is most often phonetically written, so the reader is able to pronounce the words the way they are written.

I have tried to put together a table of reference for the reader based on the IAST convention. The examples of Sanskrit words in the table below are from within the book.

IAST Transliteration Symbols	Sounds Like	Sanskrit Example
a A	the letter 'u' in the word 'but'	gajānanaṃ
ā Ā	the letter 'a' in the word 'father'	gajānanaṃ
i I	the letter 'i' in the word 'sit'	sevitaṃ

IAST Transliteration Symbols	Sounds Like	Sanskrit Example
ī Ī	the letters 'ee' in the word 'sweet'	īsāvasyaṃ
u U	the letter 'u' in the word 'cushion'	guru
ū Ū	the letters 'oo' in the word 'cool'	bhūta
e E	the letters 'ay' in the word 'say'	manorame
ai Ai	the letters 'igh' in the word 'high'	aiṃ
o O	the letter 'o' in the word 'nose'	govinda
au Au	the letters 'ow' in the word 'owl'	tannau
ṛ Ṛ	the letters 'ri' in the word 'rig'.	kṛsna
ṃ Ṃ (Indicates the vowel is nasal and the dot below is used to distinguish it from the ordinary consonant 'm'.)	the letter 'm' in the word 'come'	sevitaṃ
ḥ Ḥ (Indicates the vowel is aspirated and the dot under is used to distinguish it from the ordinary consonant 'h'.)	An aspirated 'h' sound. But, if the same 'h' comes after a vowel as in aḥ, or iḥ, then the vowel is repeated after the aspirated 'h' sound. If we were to pronounce it in English, then it would simply be 'aha' or 'ihi'	namaḥ or śantiḥ

IAST Transliteration Symbols	Sounds Like	Sanskrit Example
’	An apostrophe indicates that a letter has been dropped. In the example, the words ‘So’ + ‘aham’ combine to make one word. It is pronounced as ‘soham’, completely dropping the short vowel ‘a’ before the ‘h’	so’ham
K	the letter ‘k’ in the word ‘skill’	sūryakoti
Kh	the aspirated version of the letter ‘k’	mukha
kṣ	pronounced like ‘k + ṣ = ksh’	kṣetra
G	the letter ‘g’, as in the word ‘go’	sadgamaya
gh	the aspirated version of the letter ‘g’	ghana
ṅ	the letter ‘ng’ as in the word ‘sing’	pādapaṅkajam
C	the letters ‘ch’ in the word ‘achieve’	caturvidhama
Ch	the aspirated version of the letter ‘c’	chatraṁ
J	the letter ‘j’ in the word ‘jane’	jiva
Jh	the letter ‘dge’, in the word ‘hedge’	jhale
Jñ	the letter ‘gn’ as in the word ‘igneous’	jñanandamayaṁ

IAST Transliteration Symbols	Sounds Like	Sanskrit Example
ṭ Ṭ	the letter 't' as in the word 'sat'	puṣṭivardhanam
ṭh Ṭh	the aspirated version of the letter 'ṭ'	
ḍ Ḍ	the letter 'd' as in the word 'dry'	taḍāsanā
ḍh Ḍh	the aspirated version of the letter 'ḍ'	
ṇ Ṇ	the letters 'ng' in the word 'king'	sarvāṇgāsana
t T	the letter 'th' as in the word 'maths'	tamas
Th	the aspirated version of the letter 't'	tathā
D	the letter 'd' in the word 'did'	kundalini
Dh	the aspirated version of the letter, 'd'	dhīmahi
N	the letter 'n' in the word 'never'	niṛvighnaṁ
P	the letter 'p' in the word 'pit'	pitru
Ph	the letters, 'ph' in the word 'upheaval'. Note that it does not have the sound that the letter 'f' makes	phalam
B	the letter 'b' as in the word 'big'	balam
Bh	the aspirated version of the letter 'b'	bhavet
M	the letter 'm' in the word 'much'	matru

IAST Transliteration Symbols	Sounds Like	Sanskrit Example
y	the letter 'y' as in the word 'young', but never as a consonant in the word 'gypsy'	yoga
R	the letter 'r' in the word 'road'	arai
L	the letter 'l' in the word 'luck'	kamalaṁ
V	the letter 'v' in the word 'voice' or the letter 'w' in the word 'Swahili' Note: In Devanagari script, the sounds associated with the English letters 'w' and 'v' are allophones, so the letter 'v' could be used interchangeably	veda or swaha
ś Ś	the letters 'sh' in the word 'shallow'	śanti
ṣ Ṣ	the letter 'sh' in the word 'shove'	upaniṣhad
s S	the letter 's' in the word 'so'	smaranāt
h H	the letter 'h' in the word 'house'	saha

References for the information on IAST:

http://learnsanskrit.org
http://santanadharma.wikia.com
https://en.wikipedia.org/wiki/International_Alphabet_of_Sanskrit_Transliteration
http://www.markfoster.net/rn/iast.pdf

Information on the Chants and FAQs

Shlokas or chants are mental tools used in Hinduism to condition the mind. The effect it has on the soul is legendary. Much can and has been written and said about the positive effects of chanting. Chanting helps calm down the mind, focus better on the problem at hand and handle situations with emotional strength.

This book is written specifically for people who have very little time and who are not conversant in Tamil/Sanskrit, but would still like to chant and experience its benefits. It attempts to draw analogies with real-life situations to help understand the true meaning behind the Hindu shlokas and how they are used.

If you are reading this book, I think it's safe to assume you've finished school. You will certainly remember how we memorised nursery rhymes. One of the best ways was to break it into small chunks, understand the meaning and then keep repeating it in our minds with a particular rhythm till we were able to say it by rote. Chants are memorised the same way. The shlokas detailed in this book are very simple to read and remember.

Saying prayers before starting the day is like the process that precedes the start of any project in a company. This is when one sits down calmly and spends time evaluating different scenarios and decisions we think will make the project successful. Chanting these shlokas ensures that the negative energy trapped inside us is released and replaced with positive energy and strength to face the challenges of the world for that day.

Chanting is NOT a magic wand. Problems do not get solved just by chanting. You will need to make the effort to solve the problem, and then leave the rest to the will of the Universe. When we chant we develop the patience to let things unfold. It moves our focus from the problem to the pronunciation of the chant. This calms the mind.

The chants in this book can equip you for situations that are not foreseeable — otherwise called life. This book can help make you — child or adult — stronger in body and mind. It will help provide a new meaning to faith and devotion.

What are these chants?

With repetition, these shlokas or chants are tools used to condition the mind. The power of intent and positive affirmation helps you to reach your target.

In the words of Gautama Buddha, 'All that we are is the result of what we have thought. If a man speaks or acts with an evil thought, pain follows him. If a man speaks or acts with a pure thought, happiness follows him, like a shadow that never leaves him.' The key here is to stay positive. Some activities that will help you remain positive are:

- Believe in yourself — no matter what the situation is, remind yourself that you are capable of tackling it.
- Remind yourself to feel grateful for whatever you have.

- Eat healthy.
- Stay fit and active.
- Follow your passion.
- Move away from negative vibes and energy. Remember what Mahatma Gandhi said: 'I will not let anyone walk through my mind with their dirty feet.'

Is there any difference between shlokas, stotras and mantras?

In short, there are differences, but it is important not to get confused with the deeper meanings of these words and forget the real spiritual significance of these verses, be it a mantra or stotra. In this book, all the chants have been given a uniform nomenclature called — shloka. If there is a specific name for the verse, then it has been mentioned.

How will chanting shlokas solve my problems?

We are living in times where every act requires scientific explanation and analytical thinking. Nobody wants to simply 'accept' and perform an action because it is a trodden path. There is this burning desire to constantly reinvent the wheel to suit one's own comfort. Fair enough! So let's try putting it in those terms.

Repeating a sacred chant takes your mind away from the problem at hand temporarily, so also helping concentration. It is like giving your mind a short vacation from what is stressing you. So, after that vacation, when you come back to reality to face the problem, it helps you to focus better on it with a clear head. Do this often enough, and the ability to focus at will becomes second nature. It's just practice.

As another example, when you listen to music of your liking, does it not take you to a different zone? You feel elevated just by listening to the music. Perhaps it simply reminds you of happy times and that association helps reset the mind to its normal state.

Chanting is similar. It helps reset the mind to the equilibrium necessary for acting rationally rather than emotionally.

I believe in a higher power but do not like rituals of any kind in religion. Can I still chant?

The short answer is, yes, you can chant the shlokas, even if you do not believe in rituals.

Swami Chinmayananda once said, 'I also thought that religion meant ritualism. I never knew there was a science to it, that ritualism was just a bark. The outer bark of the great tree that shelters the whole community. The bark is necessary for the tree. But the bark is not the tree.' Ritualism does not encompass religion. Following the path of goodness, honesty, humility and even devotion to one's own job, is religion.

Which shlokas should I chant?

There are thousands. But the ones in this book are quick and easy to chant. If you're already chanting some specific shlokas, you should continue to do so, but you may want to add these to your repertoire.

How often should I chant?

Although there is no prescribed number of times to chant, repeated iterations will ensure that the sound and vibrations activate the positive energy in your body.

Generally, practising a shloka in each session over forty days will ensure that it is memorised well and that you have found the ability to concentrate on something other than your problems.

I get distracted while chanting. What should I do?

It is true that it is very difficult to focus thoughts on a particular shloka or even pray when one is disturbed or anxious. Have you noticed how heaving a big sigh when we are tense helps tremendously to alleviate the stress, even if it is only for a temporary period? The scientific reason apart, it makes you feel better, does it not?

Given below is a method to inhale and exhale while combining the chant with every breath:

1. Inhale deeply through your nose. While inhaling, say the chant in your mind and focus on your breath. For example, chant 'oṁ ṇama ṣivāya' in your mind, and breathe in as you do.
2. Exhale or breathe out through your nostrils. Chant oṁ ṇama ṣivāya again in your mind as you breathe out.

Breathing out will deflate your chest and breathing in will inflate your chest. When the focus is on the breath and its natural rhythm, you will find that you will not get that distracted. Try this method with shorter shlokas till you become used to the pronunciation and rhythm.

Useful tip: If you have a blocked nose, it's all right to breathe through your mouth. But try not to make it a habit. Breathing through the nose is more natural and calming.

Also, remember to switch off your phone before you sit down to chant. You'll be glad you did!

When should I chant?

Most people find that morning is the best time, probably because we're fresh and ready to start the day. If you find mornings are too busy to chant properly, set aside some time in the evening after your daily chores are finished, such as just before you go to bed.

Where should I chant?

Chanting can be done in any place as long as the environment evokes the correct thoughts.

Some places to avoid are probably the bedroom, bathroom and crowded public areas where the chances of distraction are more.

Sit in a comfortable position before you can begin chanting.

Do give these shlokas the due respect they deserve. Don't chant them while lying in bed or in the bathroom. It will not have the desired benefits.

Is it okay to chant more than one shloka at a time?

When we try out something new for a baby, we usually try it one at a time, since we do not know the effects it will have. Similarly, focusing on one shloka at a time will ensure that it gets your full attention. Get used to the pronunciation and include it into your routine before taking on more chants.

Why do I have to learn another language to pray? Can I not just pray in the language I am used to?

The shlokas in this book are in either Sanskrit or Tamil, two of the most ancient languages in the world. Learning a new language has many benefits — for instance, it has been proven that learning a new language slows brain ageing — and can only do more good than any harm. That being said, if you feel that you can only pray in your own language, then do so. For the benefit of those people not very familiar with Sanskrit or Tamil, the shlokas provided in this book are short enough to memorise.

Is it okay if I don't get the pronunciation right?

A name identifies a person. It is who you are. Isn't it important to people that their name is pronounced right? Would they not painstakingly correct someone to ensure that it has been said correctly?

Getting the pronunciation of a shloka right might be difficult at first, but it is desirable, as many shlokas are designed to create a particular 'sound' within you. Care has been taken in this book to ensure that the words are written correctly so that the pronunciation is right. Making the effort to learn the correct pronunciation will help you get the rich benefits of the chant. Following the pronunciation guides in this book should get you to that point pretty quickly with practice.

Do I have to clean the altar?

Just as a clean desk helps you think clearly and organise your thoughts, having a clean altar helps you chant more effectively.

Does fasting help?

Our ancestors may have at least partially seen fasting as a way to maintain health. The social structures of the time also made it much easier to fast often. Now, with both partners typically working and many cases of diabetes and stomach issues, it is strongly recommended that you do not go about with an empty stomach for a long time.

Eating a balanced diet is generally recommended. Ensure you eat well enough so that you are not distracted either by your hunger pangs or by an overloaded stomach.

Many people find that eating a fruit before a chanting session helps them concentrate better.

Should I avoid onion and garlic in food?

Onions and garlic are known to have medicinal properties. There is good evidence that consuming them improves cardiovascular health. That said, consuming onion and garlic before chanting can cause discomfort because their strong odour can be distracting, and they also occasionally cause flatulence. Therefore, minimal consumption is recommended.

Should I avoid non-vegetarian food?

Though a vegetarian diet is often recommended for health and spirituality, switching to it is up to you.

In general, foods that are rich in oils, fat and masalas are to be avoided. Saatvik food is easily digested, thus helping maintain a clear head for concentration and memorising shlokas.

Is making an offering while praying necessary?

Don't panic if you can't make kozhukattais (modaks) for Vinayakar Chaturthi! These customs are man-made. If a banana is all you have to offer, then a banana is enough.

Do I need to visit a temple?

Our ancestors lived at a time when their social lives were dependent on religious activities. Visiting temples ensured that they would meet like-minded people and friendships grew that way. A temple is also a place filled with positive vibes and energy. However, it is not absolutely necessary to visit temples to resolve your problems. In this book, the names of temples that you might like to visit have been provided after each shloka.

Why do we need to pray to so many Gods in Hinduism?
Sometimes when we think of some famous people we are reminded of one specific attribute we wish to possess or emulate: we wish to be wealthy like Bill Gates, compassionate like Mother Teresa, or have inner strength and conviction like Mahatma Gandhi. It is easier to follow a path that has been trodden by people whom we admire, isn't it? Hinduism accepts this as a valid approach and encourages it.

Hinduism is a flexible, fulfilling and easy-to-follow religion when understood deeply. To make things easier to understand and goals easier to strive towards, Hinduism has a deity for every admirable human attribute. Before the Internet and the advent of media, our ancestors told stories about Gods and Goddesses to encourage good thoughts and actions. For instance, stories about Hanuman crossing the mighty ocean to meet Sita, or carrying the Sanjeevani Mountain to cure the wounded, speaks of His courage and strength. The association of thoughts helps us mere mortals overcome the temporary challenges we face in our lives. Similarly, legends like these about the different Gods and Goddesses help people understand that they are not alone in what they are going through and that there is always a way out of problems.

While there are many Gods and Goddesses in Hinduism and many more shlokas than that, it is important to not lose focus on the goal, which is to regain composure of a disturbed mind through the chanting of shlokas. It is not absolutely necessary to visit temples to resolve your problems, but doing so would at the very least help you understand that you are not alone in facing a problem. If you are happy with praying to just one God or chanting just one shloka, then that is fine.

Is chanting a lifestyle change?

At most, it's a small investment of a few minutes at a comfortable part of the day. In any case, change can be good! Embracing the right type of change transforms the body, mind and soul. If having to chant means you need to get up half an hour earlier, eat a little healthier, drink more water, or look at your phone less, why is that a bad thing? This kind of change is easier to embrace than you'd think!

A Tip to Get Started

Chanting is only hard if you do not have the correct mind-set for it and if you are not used to the language. Here's a tip to get you started. There are some tasks in your daily routine that are mundane, but need to be done. Upload digital versions of the chants onto your smart phone, save it according to each task in your routine, like 'Cooking', 'Driving', 'Gym' or 'Yoga', and listen to them while carrying out those tasks. This way you accomplish the task and are able to listen to the chant repeatedly.

Shlokas to Improve Emotional and Mental Health

People in control of their emotions generally have better mental health as they are able to confidently handle the challenges and difficulties that come their way. They have the ability to put out emotional fires and caress their burns back to normal faster.

According to the World Health Organisation, mental health can be defined as, 'A state of wellbeing in which every individual realises his or her own potential, can cope with the normal stresses of life, can work productively and fruitfully, and is able to make a contribution to her or his community. Health is a state of complete physical, mental and social wellbeing and not merely an absence of disease or infirmity.'

Inner strength to handle difficult situations is achievable by anybody. A positive attitude towards life, the ability to have good relationships and self-esteem are all prerequisites for mental resilience. This kind of strength requires effort and practice. It's like training in the gym — the first few days are the most difficult. After that it is progressively easier as you become aware of your strengths and weaknesses. However, here, there's also the additional factor of dealing with other people's emotions.

It is extremely important to shelve negative thoughts and focus on the goal at hand to be able to excel at any task. We often encounter negative thoughts when a difficult or challenging situation occurs. These thoughts occur to everybody, but the emotionally strong person is one who can come out of it faster and find a solution to the problem at hand. This list of examples will probably sound familiar to you:

- 'Oh gosh! Where do I even begin to handle the problem? There are so many obstacles.'
- 'I wish I could calm my mind. I need peace!'
- 'I am so scared! What do I do now?'
- 'I wish I had a good partner to help me through this.'
- 'Nobody loves me. I have so many friends, yet I feel lonely.'
- 'I feel so guilty. I should not have let that happen.'
- 'I need more money to be able to afford this.'
- 'I am so hurt. I truly did not expect that person to treat me like that.'
- 'I feel so lost. I don't know where I belong!'
- 'I feel starved. I wish I had more food.'
- 'Why does that person always put me down for my lack of knowledge?'
- 'This is a tough decision to make. I don't even know what my choices are.'
- 'I wish I had done better in school! I want to excel in education.'
- 'I wish I had the courage to say no.'

In this section, you'll find some examples of the challenges most people face, some simple advice on dealing with them better, and then a set of powerful chants that will further strengthen your efforts.

Creative Ways to Overcome Obstacles

> 'We are kept from our goal, not by obstacles, but by a clear path to a lesser goal.'
>
> – *Bhagavad Gita*

There are times in our lives when we feel like we're constantly running into obstacles. There are, of course, some you can't control. A well-trained mind is able to take these in its stride and find another way. But often obstacles are simply feedback about the way you're going about things. If you're able to stop, examine and quickly correct your approach, then that's a healthy, resilient mind, and you're very likely going to reach the goals you've set. However, if you dwell on each obstacle without recognising why it's there, you'll find that more and more of them somehow keep coming your way.

A couple wanted to immigrate to Canada for better prospects, so they put in their application. As with any immigration process, it took longer than two years. Their minds were on their lives after immigrating. Their hearts were already in Canada. For the two years that they were in India, everything seemed to be delayed. Everything seemed to be taking longer. But these were not obstacles. This was just the state of mind that the couple was in. They were already living in the future in their minds, which did not let them deal with the present properly.

Here are some simple suggestions that could help the couple out:

Align and set goals: Remember how important short-term and long-term goals are while planning a project at work? Well, life is no different. Align goals with your partner and set them for the next five, ten and fifteen years. Revisit them constantly. Goals might change but the habit of goal-setting should not.

Have a game plan: All right, now you have a goal — but how do you get there? Plan! Plan! Plan! It will save you time, money and energy in the long run. How much time will it take to fulfil your goal, what will it cost, and what resources will you need?

Consult, but with caution: When we take on something new, it is always a good practice to talk to someone who is experienced in that subject or a trusted confidant whom you can use as a sounding board. However, when it comes to gauging trustworthiness and merit, all you can do is develop your instinct for it.

Delegate responsibilities: No matter what your future plans are, your current job provides your bread and butter at the moment, and your current life provides you fulfilment. You cannot afford to lose focus on that. Divide your responsibilities with your partner to handle the future as well as the present. If you are handling it alone, you should expect unpleasant compromises. Take them in your stride while also attempting to minimise them.

Clean-up day: Set aside one day of the week to clean up your emails, thoughts and ideas. Take a step back from everything you're doing and find your bearings.

Evaluate your progress: Take a little time periodically to determine how you are doing with your plan.

Think proactively: Planning for contingencies is important. This is being realistic, not pessimistic, and will help you handle a problem even before it can come up.

Plan for success: This should be your mantra. Get up in the morning with clearly defined goals for the day. Plan for success for the day's goals.

Learn to be comfortable with having limited control and foresight. To be able to handle and overcome obstacles that we didn't foresee, we need mental balance. The following chants can help you with that.

Shloka 1 to overcome obstacles

Chant this Ganesha Bheej mantra to sow the seeds for positive change in all that you do. This chant's vibrations will empower you to take on any task without fear or trepidation.

oṁ gam ganapataye namaḥ

Meaning

Salutations to Lord Ganesha, the leader of Ganas!

Shloka 2 to overcome obstacles

Chant this Ganesha mantra to shed your ego and request the Almighty to ensure that the path you have taken is the path for success.

vakratuṇḍa mahākāya
sūryakoṭi samaprabha
nirvighnam kuru me deva
sarva kāryeśusarvadā

Meaning

Oh! One with the curved trunk and huge body, who is shining like a million suns, I pray that all my tasks and endeavours be removed of obstacles always.

Shloka 3 to overcome obstacles

Ganesha is thought to be the remover of obstacles. It is customary to pray to Ganesha before the beginning of any important undertaking. Chant this to clear negative thoughts that are crowding your mind.

gajānanaṁ bhūtagaṇādi sevitaṁ
kapittha jambūphalasāra bhakṣitam
umāsutaṁ śoka vināśakāraṇaṁ
namāmi vighneśvara pādapaṅkajam

Meaning

Oh! One who has an elephant face and who is served by Bhuta and other Ganas,
One who eats the core of kapitha and jambu fruits,
Son of Uma and destroyer of sorrows,
I salute you at your lotus feet, oh remover of obstacles.

Devotional songs

The Ganesha Pancharathnam, sung by Bharat Ratna M.S. Subbulakshmi, makes for an exhilarating four minutes. There are many such devotional songs on Ganesha, but one that is very uplifting is called *Gananayakaya,* sung by Shankar Mahadevan. A masterpiece!

Temples to visit

You might find the Ganesha temple in Thiruvalanchuzhi interesting. The Ganesha here is known as Swetha Vinayagar or Vellai Pillaiyaar. The name comes from the following legend.

While the Asuras and Devas were churning the ocean for the nectar of immortality, the only thing that kept coming out was poison. This was because the Devas had forgotten to pray to Lord Ganesha. Lord Indra realised this mistake and quickly made a 'Norai Pillaiyaar', or Froth Ganesha, out of the froth of the ocean waves. Lord Ganesha was pleased, and nectar finally started emerging out of the ocean waves.

Find Your Peace and Keep It

> 'The peace of God is with them whose mind and souls are in harmony, who are free from desire and wrath, and who know their own soul.'
>
> – *Bhagavad Gita*

We make all kinds of efforts to ensure that there is peace in the heart and home. We try Feng Shui, religious practices like yagnas, spa treatments, and so on. We also find that their effects are fleeting, so we just move from one temporary fix to the next.

A couple had just moved to a new home in a new country. Both had exciting careers: the woman was a working professional and the man's job required him to travel a lot. They had a child who was healthy and doing very well in school. A peaceful, happy family.

Then, one day, their maid suddenly stopped coming without notice and all that peace came crashing down. Lunches weren't packed, there was no babysitter for the child, the wife was not pleased about scaling back from her job and the husband was unwilling to reschedule work to better suit his wife.

While the solution to the above problem is very family-specific, the important thing to remember is that the entire family would need to be mindful that every member needs to be ready to make compromises and sacrifices. There's no quick-fix solution to this problem.

Determine the source of your energy: There are two types of energy: one that fuels your positive outlook and makes you feel great, and another that drains you and makes you feel tired all the time. Determine the sources for each. Negative energy could come from anything — a toxic relationship, an unorganised home, taking on more tasks than you can handle, or even simply eating the wrong type of food. Positive energy comes from fewer sources. Unfortunately we feel its absence more than we feel its presence! Don't we seldom appreciate good food till we eat the wrong kind and get a stomach ache?

Let it go: Thoughts have this uncanny ability to linger, even when you want to be done with it — specially the type of thoughts and feelings that hurt. Pain suffered in past situations can persist and destroy peace of mind. We need to let things go, and make peace with the past. We all need a method that helps put the brakes on cerebral traffic. Unclog your mind with these basic chants.

Shloka 1 for peace

An elephant's eyes convey a feeling of absolute peace and compassion. Chanting this hymn with dedication and focusing on the eyes of Lord Ganesha is sure to bring success in the form of peace and prosperity.

oṁ sumukhāya namaḥ

Meaning

Salutations to the one with a pleasant face.

Shloka 2 for peace

The Goddess of eternal peace and love for her devotees is Kamakshi. This deity is depicted in the yogic pose of padmasana, signifying peace and harmony with the world and within.

om śāntimatyai namaḥ

Meaning

Salutations to the peaceful Mother.

Shloka 3 for peace

Chant this mantra, which is from *Taittiriya* and the *Katha Upanishad*, to realise peace in togetherness.

oṁ saha nāvavatu
saha nau bhunaktu
saha vīryaṁ karavāvahai
tejasvi_nāvadhītamastu mā vidviṣāvahai
oṁ śāntiḥ śāntiḥ śāntiḥ

Meaning

Loosely translated, it means:

Om, may we all be protected,
May we all be nourished,
May we work together with great energy

May our intellect be sharpened (may our study be effective)
Let there be no animosity amongst us
Om, peace (in me), peace (in nature), peace (in divine forces)

Shloka 4 for peace

The serene face of Lord Buddha is what comes to mind when we think of peace. This is considered the holiest of chants in Tibet:

oṁ mani padme hūṁ

Meaning

This shloka can be translated as: 'Praise to the jewel in the lotus.'

In Sanskrit, mani is jewel, and padma is lotus. It is believed that all human beings have an inherent holiness in them. It is through the practice of holy thoughts, speech and action that one can transform the impure to pure.

His Holiness Tenzin Gyatso, the Fourteenth Dalai Lama of Tibet, explains this chant's meaning: 'Dependence on the (holy) practice which is an indivisible union of method and wisdom, you can transform your impure body, speech and mind into the pure body, speech and mind of a Buddha.' That is, practise what you preach and believe that you have it in you to find your inner peace and, hence, yourself.

Devotional songs

The Kamakshi stotram by Shri Adi Shankaracharya has many different enchanting names that challenge one's memory. Memorising them will surely build your patience, resulting in the inner peace that comes with building patience.

The other songs that bring a lot of peace because of their lilting music are 'Om Gan Ganapataye Namah', sung by Shankar Mahadevan, 'Om Mani Padme Hum with Prayers' by His Holiness, The Dalai Lama, and the Shanti mantra by Ravi Shankar and George Harrison.

Temples to visit

The Chintamani temple in Pune is a Ganesha temple. This temple is the fifth temple in a set of eight temples that are covered on a pilgrimage called Ashta Vinayaka Yatra (pilgrimage of eight Ganeshas). The Ganesha gets his name 'Chintamani' from two different legends. One legend is elaborated here.

Lord Brahma felt very restless and his mind was full of troubling thoughts. He then decided to meditate in Theur, the place where the temple is now situated. Lord Ganesha removed all the worries that Lord Brahma had and calmed his mind. Since Lord Ganesha removed his worrisome thoughts ('chinta', in Sanskrit), he was named Chintamani.

Other temples that can be visited are the Kamakshi temple in Kanchipuram, sanctified by the holy presence of Sage Shankaracharya, and the Akilandeswari temple in Tiruvaanai Kaaval. Bodhgaya, in Buddhagaya, Bihar, is a beautiful Buddhist temple built by King Ashoka. The temple is an architectural gem and is a wonderful place to start meditation practice and find peace.

Don't Lose Your Mind, Lose Your Haste

'Little by little, through patience and repeated effort, the mind will become stilled in the Self.'

– Bhagavad Gita

As the saying goes, 'Haste makes waste'. In this fast-paced life, filled with a good measure of stress, very often we find ourselves doing so many things in a hurry. This, unfortunately, leads to forgetfulness. How often have we found ourselves looking everywhere for an object, only to end up finding it safely stored away somewhere?

Krishna had recently bought a home in Chennai. At the time of closing, he was given a sale deed, which he stashed away safely. Buying this home was a great accomplishment for an up-and-coming professional in his late twenties. He worked in a very demanding job at an IT company that required him to spend many late nights in office. Two years and three transfers later, an email from the building association requested that he upload his sale deed to their website, so that they could apply for property tax assessment.

Elated that they were taking on the responsibility from the builder, he asked his wife, Ratna, to upload the document, which she went about looking for immediately.

Two hours later, she was still looking.

She made a frantic call to her husband, who was travelling, and explained to him that the sale deed was missing.

Krishna returned early to look for the files. Ratna said, 'I know that this must be done, but please have dinner first.' Krishna, fuming, retorted, 'The sale deed is missing and you want me to have dinner?' Ratna looked at him calmly and said, 'I know this is worrying, but let's stay calm. We'll find it. We can't lose our mind over something like this.'

After dinner and a small prayer, the couple resumed their search.

Within an hour, they had found the sale deed.

Now, there are two ways to look at this.

- They found it because they believed in miracles.
- They found it because they calmed down and believed in themselves.

But both were right, because miracles do happen when we believe in ourselves!

Shloka to find something that is lost

Durga or Amman is the Goddess of strength and courage in south India and in West Bengal. She brings those qualities to all those who focus on any of Her forms. Chant this Tamil shloka of Amman to calm your nerves:

oṁ araikāsu ammane potri

Meaning

Loosely translated, this shloka means, 'Salutations and victory to Araikasu Amman.'

Shloka for awareness at all times

Chant this shloka as soon as you get up every morning. This is sure to calm your mind. Open your hands, look into your palms, and chant this shloka:

karāgre vasate lakṣmiḥ karamadhye sarasvati
karamūle tu govindaḥ prabhāte karadarśanam

Meaning

On the palm of the hand dwells Devi Lakshmi and in the middle of the hand, dwells Saraswati
At the base of the hand dwells Lord Govinda
(With this thought) Look at your hands in the morning

Devotional songs

Chanting the Lalitha Ashtothram as sung by T.S. Ranganthan is bound to give you a tranquil mind in less than ten minutes.

Temples to visit

Shri Arai Kaasu Amman temple is located in Rathinamangalam, near Chennai. One of the many forms that the Goddess took was that of Pragadhambal Amman. The story goes that there was once a king in Puddukotai who lost an important document and, when he prayed to Pragadhambal Amman, he found it almost immediately. Pleased, the king ordered a new kind of silver coinage for his kingdom — semi-circular, with an image of the Goddess on one side. From then onwards the Amman came to be called Arai Kaasu Amman, which means 'half-coin goddess', and people started to pray to Her for the recovery of lost items.

The main idol is surrounded by one hundred and seven Amman shrines across the temple, each in a different posture.

Attack Anxiety Before It Can Attack You

> 'Fear not what is not real, never was and never will be. What is real always was and cannot be destroyed.'
>
> – *Bhagavad Gita*

Imagine a life without fear. No fear of becoming poor. No fear of death. No fear of accidents. No fear of terrorism. No fear of anything. You are one with the world and accept life as it comes. That would be wonderful. But let's get real. This can only happen in a fairy tale. Real world challenges are true levellers. They're like a thermostat that sets things at the optimum level of comfort for your health.

For some people, anxiety and fear act as catalysts for achieving greater heights. This, unfortunately, is just an illusion. Once they have conquered one fear this way, another fear will appear. It is like an infection with no cure. The only way that you can learn how to use fear healthily is by accepting that you cannot control everything in your life. It helps to believe that whatever happens in your life does so for a reason.

□□

Meena was engulfed with fear for herself, her child and the life that she had so carefully built along with her soul-mate. This fear had been triggered off by news about a local train crash on TV. It was the train that Meena's husband would have taken, had he not by chance decided to take the next one.

What if something happened to him? How will I face the world alone? Irrational ideas started to form in her mind. Sure enough, it soon turned into a cobweb of thoughts and snowballed into something big. Suddenly, she just couldn't stop the avalanche of tears that followed.

Meena decided to do something about this anxiety attack. She asked her husband to send her a text message as soon as he reached his workplace. This way, her anxiety was alleviated about his safety en route to work. Meena's husband, who was very understanding, did this for his wife gladly.

As Meena did, the best way to handle anxiety sometimes is to catch the anxious bull by its horns and find a solution. Here are a few tips on handling anxious thoughts.

Be your own devil's advocate: Sometimes the best way to challenge anxious thoughts is to ask questions of yourself. Is this fear really legitimate? What must I do to overcome this fear? Can I distract myself with a book, or perhaps listen to some music that I like?

Change focus: Anxiety is often fed greatly by laziness and time to spare. Use your time well and focus on things that you like doing.

Exercise: Enough cannot be said on the well-known and proven positive effects of exercise on the body and mind. Exercise in almost any form can be a stress-reliever. It releases feel-good endorphins and distracts you from your worries.

Take a break: If you find that you are getting anxious very quickly and often, then perhaps it is time for a break. Take a short vacation to recharge your batteries.

List out your anxieties: Sometimes when you write down your thoughts, their intensity reduces and slowly disappears. List out what is worrying you and slowly strike each one of them out, as if you are striking them out from your mind.

Shloka to overcome anxiety

Shri Anjaneya (Hanuman) is the embodiment of courage and strength to overcome adversities, irrational fears and challenges that may come our way. Chant this shloka to overcome fear:

buddhir balam yaśo dhairyam
nirbhayatvam arogatām
ajāḍyam vāk paṭutvam ca
hanumat smaraṇāt bhavet

Meaning

Intelligence, strength, fame, courage,
Fearlessness, disease-free health,
Activeness, articulateness, will all last forever
If you meditate on Lord Hanuman at all times

Devotional songs

The full Hanuman Chalisa sung by M.S. Subbulakshmi takes about ten minutes. Sing and chant this shloka to condition your mind to face the challenges of the world and build the courage to speak your mind.

Temples to visit

The Ashtamsa Shri Varada Anjaneya temple is located in the Peelamedu suburb of Coimbatore. The temple has eight special features that make it stand apart from other Anjaniputhra temples. For instance, Shri Anjaneya is normally portrayed with his hands folded in prayer to Shri Rama, or carrying a mountain while flying, but this deity is different. Here, the Lord's abhaya hastha (right hand) is raised as if to protect his devotees from their fears, while his left hand holds a mace, gadha, to destroy not only the five negative attributes that give room for fear — lust, anger, greed, infatuation and jealousy — but the external negativity that surrounds humans. The deity also faces the west, towards the Sanjeevani Mountain, known for its medicinal plants. Rather atypically, this Anjaneya's tail is fully visible, whereas it is usually hidden behind his back.

Legend has it that this long tail houses the nine planets or the navagrahas, so praying to the tail alone gets rid of the bad effects that the planets may have on you.

Lose That Fear; Live in the Now

> 'There is neither this world nor the world beyond nor happiness for the one who doubts.'
>
> – *Bhagavad Gita*

There are times when you experience fear for your spouse's wellbeing. These fears usually get increasingly irrational unless they are countered healthily.

The general fears that Meena went through in the previous section's example, is what every person who is financially and emotionally dependent on their partner will go through at some point. Of course, there are prayers that make us emotionally strong but there are also practical things that one must do in order to feel less anxious. For instance, if a woman decides to take time off work after having had a baby, here are some things she can do:

Plan for your sabbatical: Treat your break away from work as a planned sabbatical. Save for yourself some money that you can use to pamper yourself, so you don't feel the need to ask your spouse for money every time. This requires both your spouse and you to be very diligent about how much you put away every month.

Minimalistic living: If the wife gives up her career to be a stay-at-home mom, care must be taken about finances. Live within your means. Ask yourself questions about your lifestyle before every substantial purchase. Do I really need that second car? What creative ways can I find to manage with one? Is that gym membership really required? I could instead go for walks, or better still, buy the basic equipment, which probably equals the cost of two evening dresses? Cut your costs and save! The more you save, the more secure you will feel.

Develop your passion: Taking care of your kids is important, but not at the cost of your individuality. Pursue that passion which you could not while you were working.

***Work out*:** It is said that exercising releases positive hormones and dispels negative thoughts. Find creative ways to get fitter.

Enjoy yourself: This time that you have is precious. Not many people can afford to take time off. Enjoy it and stop feeling guilty. If somebody is judging you, let them. It is their loss that they waste their own time thinking negatively. Celebrate your gain and bury their loss.

Shloka that women can chant

The Kathyayani Devi mantra is for sustaining a marriage, protecting a husband from harm, and can also be chanted by anyone who wants to get married.

kāthyāyani mahāmāye mahāyoginyadhīśvari
nanda gopasutaṁ devipatiṁ me kuru te namaḥ

Meaning

Kathyayani, greatest of all magicians, Goddess of all yoginis,
May Nandakumara become my husband.
Prostrations unto Thee

Shloka that men can chant

The Patni Prāpti Durga shloka below is sure to bring peace to the confused mind.

patnīṁ manoramāṁ dehi manovṛtānu sāriṇīm
tāriṇīm durga saṁsāra sāgarasya kulodbhavāma

Meaning

O Devi! Please give me the wife who is pleasing and helpful and can make my mind happy,
Who can cross the most difficult worldly ocean and who comes from a good family

Devotional songs

Memorise the Durga Pancharatnam by listening to M.S. Subbulakshmi's rendition of the song. It will take approximately four minutes. Focusing on the positive traits of Goddess Durga, the embodiment of courage and strength, will surely give you the strength to move on from your fears.

Temples to visit

Any temple will ward off unreasonable fears, but if you would like to go to a temple where the deity is Goddess

Kathyayani, then you many want to visit the one situated at Thiruveezhimizhalai, Tamil Nadu. Goddess Kathyayani is an avatar of Goddess Parvati and she is said to have been reborn and married to Lord Shiva here. This particular Goddess is the consort of the presiding deity in the Veezhinatheswarar temple, Shri Kalyanasundareswarar (also known as Mapillai Swamy, meaning Bridegroom Lord).

Married and Happily Ever After

> 'A vision of oneness develops love, a readiness to serve all and creates an attitude of forgiveness.'
>
> *– Swami Tejomayananda*

Finding a good life partner is considered an important part of adulthood across most cultures. Marriage is seen as an important beginning of a lifelong relationship that provides the basis for love and happiness in its different forms.

Marriage is a close association of two individuals. They come into the relationship from different paths of life, different lifestyles, value systems, family traditions, food habits, expectations and ideas. There is no magic wand that can be waved to make the marriage work. An abundance of compromises, innumerable sacrifices, unimaginable tolerance and tons of love is what makes a marriage. Enjoy this relationship, for not everyone is lucky to have found a soul-mate. You have.

Their honeymoon was over quite literally. Pravin and Aditi were back to the reality of house loans, car loans, education loans, managing careers, and so on. The list of financial and emotional challenges in their relationship was mounting. She could not handle the stress of juggling home and work. He was unable to handle the stress from his job and from being the primary caregiver of the family. Sound familiar?

Take a step away: Step back from the problem and realise that you are not alone. In fact, you are one of the lucky ones, as you have each other to solve the issue — as a couple. Two heads are better than one!

Leave E behind: When it comes to ego, leave the capital 'E' behind and just move forward! Most often, in relationships, a person's ego hampers finding a solution to the problem. It comes in the way of logical thinking, because you are only thinking about yourself and not the family as a whole.

Wedding or marriage?: Remember how excited you were planning your wedding? The flowers, the jewellery, the cards and invitations? Was it all for just one day of excitement? The wedding is just a day to legitimise your relationship. Remember that you have made a lifelong commitment to this relationship called marriage and must invest in it all you have.

Communicate: Clear and continuous communication is the key to any good relationship. Without communication, assumptions fill up the void and this can get dangerous and lead to more and more misunderstandings. Sit down and talk about your fears, your worries, anger or sadness, and always tell each other when and why you are happy. If your partner is not very good at communicating, then work on making him / her better at it.

Align your goals: It is normal for both people in most relationships to begin with different goals. But eventually, goals must align. The goals that each person would have had when the marriage first took place will constantly get redefined. Issues like kids, caring for elders and finances constantly realign these goals. This is nature's way. Constant communication and revisiting your priorities and wishes is important so that changing goals do not become a point of contention. Instead, it will actually make your relationship stronger.

In the great epic *Ramayana*, the relationship between Rama and Sita withstood many tests: banishment, loss of comfort, kidnapping, harassment. Sita's devotion, respect and love for Rama and his undying love for her is easy to see. The love between the two teaches us, as humans, how to keep relationships strong during troubled times, even if it means crossing oceans.

Quoting the famous poet, Kahlil Gibran:

You were born together, and together
you shall be forevermore.
You shall be together when the white wings of
death scatter your days.
Ay, you shall be together even in the silent memory of God.
But let there be spaces in your togetherness,
And let the winds of the heavens dance between you.

Shloka for a good marital life

Chant this shloka from the Devi Mahatmyam to heal marital discord.

sarvamaṅgalamāṅgalye śive
sarvārthasādhike
śaraṇye tryambake gauri nārāyaṇi
namo'stu te

Meaning

(Salutation to) You, one who is full of auspiciousness and is the consort of Lord Shiva.
You can accomplish all tasks. I surrender to you, oh the one with three eyes. We salute you, oh Gauri, oh Narayani!

Devotional songs

Chant the Ardha Nareeswara stotram by Shri Adi Shankaracharya. There is also the Shri Shiva Ardhanareeswara sthotram. S.P. Balasubramaniam's rendition will take around ten minutes.

There is a saying, 'A family that prays together, stays together.' Try incorporating songs such as 'Om Jaya Jaya Jaya Shakthi' — a Tamil song sung during the time of arathi — into your prayers. The version sung by T.S. Ranganathan is sure to bring the family closer.

Temples to visit

There are several temples that one can visit.

The Nithya Kalyana Perumal temple, located in Thiruvidenthai, Tamil Nadu, is one of the famous temples associated with marriage. The presiding deity is Shri Vishnu, in the Varaha avatar. His consort here is Lakshmi, who is called Komalavalli Thayar in this temple.

Legend has it that Sage Galava had three hundred and sixty daughters. He requested a young sage to marry his daughters. This sage married one daughter every day for an entire year. On the last day, he showed his true form: Lord Varaha (Lord Vishnu in the form of a boar).

Lord Varaha then merged all the daughters into one and placed her as his consort on his left ('idathu' in Tamil means left) knee. The place got its name, Tiruvidavendhai, from this; later on it became Thiruvidenthai.

The Lord gets the name Nithya Kalyana Perumal as he married every day (nithya – daily; kalyanam – marriage).

Other temples to visit for this purpose are:

- Thirumanancheri: This temple is situated in Nagai district, Tamil Nadu. Thirumanancheri is one of the popular temples dedicated to Lord Shiva. The deity is worshipped as Kalyanasundareshwarar and His consort, Goddess Parvati, as Kokilaambal.
- Ardhanarishvarar temple: Ardhanarishvarar is a composite form of Lord Shiva and Goddess Parvati. The deity is depicted in a half-male and half-female form, signifying that in a marriage the man and woman have equal responsibility to make it work. This temple is situated in Thiruchengode.

Finding Forever Friends

> 'A man's own self is his friend. A man's own self is his foe.'
>
> – *Bhagavad Gita*

We want things to happen now. We want friends now. We want money now. We want happiness now. We live in a world where the power of now overwhelms the power of love and friendship. Power breakfasts. Power exercise. Power naps. At the end of all this, one feels one completely lacks the power to invest time and energy in a relationship.

Friendships do not grow overnight. One needs to invest time and effort in it. Why was it so easy to get back in touch with our school or college friends on Facebook? For the simple reason that you were pushed into each other's spheres day in and day out. You shared just one world for many years.

As we grow older, finding friendships becomes more difficult. Colleagues from work are the next best thing to school or college friends, because again you share a similar world. But in this day and age, people often move to new jobs, new cities, countries, and sometimes a completely different continent.

Apart from constantly trying to find your identity, you also have to find friends — the good ones!

A couple was offered an assignment abroad. Greatly excited, the couple moved bag and baggage. New people, a different culture, a new language. They were young and up for the challenges that surrounded the expat life and reinvented themselves and adapted well.

Five years later, their jobs took them elsewhere. They said their goodbyes to their friends and went on to their next new life. This time with less enthusiasm, but nevertheless still looking forward to new experiences. They faced challenges again. They adapted, albeit a little slower.

Over the next few years, they moved twice, to two different countries. The couple became so tired with this that they began desperately looking for familiar sights and sounds. It prevented them from making new friends.

The couple blamed their situation as if it were unprecedented and unwelcome, all the time forgetting that they had chosen this lifestyle. Nothing was forced on them.

It is impossible to predict where life will take you, so we need to keep reminding ourselves that, when we choose our paths, it is up to us to make the most of it.

***Shut up, but open up*:** Sometimes the best way to overcome an inability to make new friends and surround yourself with people is to be more open — open about what others say, other cultures and other lifestyles. You don't have to make your opinion heard all the time. Learn to listen silently. It is an art!

Prepare for the rendezvous: When you go for a business meeting, do you not prepare for it? Think of all the things that you have in common with the people you are going to meet. Use social media to understand their interests. Some people may call this stalking, but I would call this market research.

The rendezvous: You will need to market yourself without being overbearing. Find common interests with the people you are meeting and see if you can do something together.

Follow-up: After any interview, it is courtesy to send a thank-you note. Be spontaneous in following up with everyone you meet and mention a desire to meet them again soon. This will be something both of you can look forward to.

Go the extra mile: If you find that you have struck a common chord with someone, go the extra mile. Wish them on their birthday / anniversary or call them over for dinner. Show that you enjoy their company. At first, it may seem like you are the one making all the effort. Maybe their need to make friends is just less than yours! So if you want a friend, you'll have to take a little trouble for it.

Shloka for better relationships

This Mahalakshmi mantra helps you understand that it takes a lot to make any relationship work. No pain, no gain! It isn't rocket science, and starts with as simple a thing as open communication. Chant the mantra below to open up the mind to the immense possibilities of a healthy relationship.

oṁ ṣrīm mahālakṣmīyai namaḥ

Meaning

Loosely translated, this shloka means, 'Salutations to Goddess Mahalakshmi.' Mahalakshmi is the Goddess of wealth, which does not only pertain to material wealth. Prosperity is also signified by good friends around you.

Devotional songs

Take five minutes to sing the Mahalakshmi Ashtakam along with the Bombay Sisters. Learn the beautiful hymn 'Namastesthu Mahaamaaye', sung by Shankar Mahadevan. It is in praise of Goddess Mahalakshmi.

Temples to visit

When there is an abundance of wealth, health and happiness, the mind establishes oneness with the divine. With this peaceful divinity, you draw more people and friends towards you. This is not to imply that only the rich make friends, but to suggest that contentment in the heart automatically allows the making of new friends.

Visit any Mahalakshmi temple to get rid of enmity in you towards people, for example, the Ashtalakshmi temple in Chennai. The temple has eight different shrines for the Goddess, all under one roof. Ashtalakshmi (meaning eight Lakshmis) gives all the different types of treasures that one needs to live as follows:

- Santhanalakshmi (Bestower of offspring)
- Vijayalakshmi (Bestower of success)
- Vidyalakshmi (Bestower of knowledge)
- Gajalakshmi (Bestower of prosperity and abundance)
- Dhanalakshmi (Bestower of wealth)

- Dhaanya Lakshmi (Bestower of food and freedom from hunger)
- Adi Lakshmi (Grants good health)
- Dhairya Lakshmi (Grants courage)

Goddess Lakshmi grants the boon of all types of achievements and wealth, and the resplendent way in which the Goddess is always dressed will fill your heart with joy.

chaos) and you will find people respect you more, simply because you respect yourself.

❑❑

Anoushka is a typical teenager. She's generally embarrassed by whatever her parents do. Being a second-generation immigrant in a Western world simply made it worse. Born in India, but raised in North America, she loved everything Indian, but was not comfortable sharing that with her friends. What would they think of her? Would she be accepted by her group if they knew she ate rotis? Would they make fun of her mom wearing a saree? However hard she tried, she was also unable to change the strong and thick Indian accent her vowels had. She was sure she got her accent from her dad, as he spoke more in English. She even sometimes found herself wishing he did not speak so much.

Although this kind of behaviour soon disappears after puberty, it takes longer in children who have moved away from their roots. Most emigrant parents try their best to ensure that their children do not lose touch with their culture, without being overbearing, but it's quite hard.

The problems that these children face are real. Here are some ways to help them.

Do not undermine their fears: Undermining their fears will only push them further away from you and your culture. Feeling accepted is an important priority when you are young and impressionable, so they will gravitate to wherever they get that.

Do not impose your beliefs: Do not force them to learn and chant the long and complicated prayers you learnt as a child. These are prayers that they don't understand or appreciate, and forcing them to recite them will only

Find Your Roots; Cherish Your Beginnings

> 'For the large-hearted, the whole world is just one family.'
>
> – *Bhagavad Gita*

Your birthday is a day to be cherished all through your life. A life that takes you through being an infant, a toddler, a teen, an adult and a senior citizen. It is on this day that your parents brought you into this wonderful world. They held your hand through all your ups and downs and let you fly when you were ready to build your own nest.

Then, there are the roots. These are what allow the tree to grow bigger and stronger. They need to be nourished frequently so that even the highest tip of the tree always remains fresh. Marriage, careers, children and more may steer you away from paths that are different from your beginnings. Embrace your roots, learn your mother tongue, love all that your culture offers (including the make them dislike the practice. To ensure that the child develops an appreciation for the religion, request the child to be present for five minutes every day while you chant small and short shlokas. Often the shlokas have some mythological stories associated with them. Tell them those stories and explain the meaning. At the very least, they will appreciate the time you spend with them. This will have a far more positive impact on the child.

Do not force them to learn the mother tongue: Don't force them to learn and speak your native language. Talk to them in your mother tongue but give them the freedom to reply in the language they are comfortable with. Language is simply a tool to communicate. So how does it matter how they say it as long as they are communicating properly with you?

Inculcate respect for other's sentiments: Ensure that the child is respectful at all times to the family's religious sentiments. Take time to explain how, most often, these religious sentiments relate to hygiene, good discipline and good habits.

Inculcate good habits: Good habits can be taught irrespective of the culture in which the child grows up. Small things like looking a person in the eye and speaking; saying thank you; and being courteous could help the child go a long way in society.

Love for one's own self: Loving yourself and your identity — where you come from, your place of birth, your ancestry and your beginnings — will bring you self-confidence, and confidence brings respect from others.

Shloka to remember our beginnings

The following verse is taken from the ancient Sanskrit scripture, the *Taittiriya Upanishad.*

mātṛu devo bhava,
pitṛu devo bhava,
ācārya devo bhava,
athithi devo bhava

Meaning

Let divinity be thy mother,
Let divinity be thy father,
Let divinity be thy teacher,
Let divinity be thy guest

Devotional songs

Reading the *Prapanna Gita* or the *Pandava Gita*, which is a collection of shlokas and hymns, is sure to help remind you of the very deep philosophy in Indian scriptures, which is that of attachment. All Indian scriptures advocate a very difficult concept to understand and practise, called attached detachment. This can be cultivated in an individual only one way — which is to experience challenges in relationships of all kinds. The *Prapanna Gita* advocates complete surrender to the Almighty.

The following verse, Verse 28, was apparently said by Gandhari (mother of the Kauravas) to Krishna, as she surrendered herself to the Lord. It is a very popular and beautiful hymn.

tvameva mātā ca pitā tvameva
tvameva bandhuśca sakhā tvameva
tvameva vidyā draviṇam tvameva
tvameva sarvam mama deva deva

Listen to 'Twameva Mata', sung by P. Unnikrishnan and Rakshita, Haripriya and Anu. It takes less than two minutes.

Temples to visit

Every Hindu family has a particular temple they regard as their 'family temple'. Sometimes these temples could be famous ones in large cities or very small ones in remote villages. Either way, do make an effort to visit your family temple at least once as an adult. It will connect you to your roots and ancestors in a beautiful way. You might also get to see your ancestral place, if that's where the temple is.

Given below is information on one family temple, Shri Aamra Vaneswarar temple in Mandurai, Trichy. The primary deity is Shri Aamra Vaneswarar and the name of his consort is Balaambikai.

Legend has it that a sage committed a grave mistake and was cursed by Lord Shiva to be born as a deer in a mango forest. The deer was born to other deer that had been demons in an earlier birth. One day, the parents of the deer left it behind. Lord Shiva and Parvati came as hunters to the forest and released the parents of the deer from their curses, fed the small deer with milk and released him also from his curse. Mandurai gets its name from this legend: 'maan' means deer, and the region was dense with mango trees.

Devotees come to this temple for relief from problems affecting their children.

Nip Guilt in the Bud

> '...Doing actions intrinsic to his being, a man avoids guilt.'
>
> – *Bhagavad Gita*

There are times in our lives when we wish we had not done or said something, especially if our actions had negative consequences. This is a common problem that everybody goes through at some point or the other. It is how we come out of these situations that make us who we are. The first thing to do would be, of course, to choose a remedial action towards the person who was wronged. The second is to ensure that you let go of your guilt.

Here are some common situations where people face guilt:

- Sangeetha suffers pangs of guilt for leaving her two-year-old in day care. She finds herself wondering if she is being a bad mother.

- Mohan's work and its pressures force him to come back home stressed out and much later than his kid's bedtime, which makes him feel guilty and stresses him out even more.
- Venkat lives in the US with his wife and family and is in a high-pressure job. His parents live in India and Venkat is their only child. He can afford to take off only two weeks a year. His guilt for not being able to take care of his aging parents bothers him on a daily basis.
- Prachi is feeling very guilty that she told on her friend to her teacher at school. The friend had an eating disorder and Prachi felt she needed help.

Whatever the type of guilt faced, effort must be taken to overcome the same. Action-oriented people overcome guilt and depression associated it much faster than others. So it is very necessary to take action and not be pulled down further into the quagmire of guilt.

Here are some simple steps to overcome guilt:

Accept the mistake and move on: The first step in overcoming guilt is to accept the mistake. This will help you overcome the emotion faster and move on with your life. Mistakes happen in everybody's life. It is how we overcome these that define us and our character. Rise above the negative emotion of guilt.

Share with someone: The best way to unburden is to share your feelings with somebody trustworthy. It also helps greatly to get a third person's perspective on a situation.

Take the necessary action: If the emotion is worthy of your time and energy and requires reparations, then the best time to do it is now. If you are guilty of an action, then find ways to compensate the person or situation that has been hurt, either monetarily or by your actions. If you find that the guilt you are facing is in fact misplaced, try to find ways to show yourself more compassion so you can heal faster.

Shloka to overcome guilt

Chant this Shiva shloka to overcome the guilt you feel for unintentional mistakes.

oṁ harāya namaḥ

Meaning

Loosely translated, this shloka means, 'Salutation to the Lord who withdraws the cosmos.' This can be understood as the Lord destroying the negative universe you've been experiencing and replacing it with one that is suitable to you. Again, this is brought about not only by chanting this shloka, but also by positive action from you.

Devotional songs

The Shiva Aparadha Kshamapana stotram, written by Shri Adi Shankaracharya, is a beautiful hymn asking for forgiveness from the Almighty for sins committed. Once forgiveness has been asked from the Almighty, we are devoid of any guilt.

The version of this shloka sung by T.S. Ranganathan takes less than nine minutes.

Temples to visit

Visit the Kapaleeshwarar temple, a temple of Lord Shiva, located in Chennai. Legend has it that, once, Lord Shiva was explaining the meaning of 'Om Nama Shivaaya' to his consort, Goddess Parvati. She was very distracted at the time and her attention was on peacocks dancing around them. Apparently Lord Shiva got so angry with her, that he cursed her to become a peacock.

Karpagambal, the residing Goddess of this temple, came here to do her penance under a tree called the Punnai tree, to invoke the blessings of the Lord and overcome her guilt at distracting the Lord. Pleased by her devotion and her penance, Lord Shiva joined her in the temple.

Attract the Right Wealth

'There is enough in the world for everybody's need and not for everybody's greed.'

– *Mahatma Gandhi*

The Universe provides enough for us to live well. We are fortunate that we have had the opportunity to be educated, have access to good clothing, a roof over our heads, and material things beyond our needs. We can only hope that the prosperity bestowed upon us is shared with the less fortunate. Giving to charitable causes is one way of contributing. The other indirect but important way is by spending less and living according to our actual needs.

A young couple had just started their married lives. Their minds were filled with desires, ambitions and needs. Both had decent jobs, but moving up in their career would take time. They were driven by material pleasures and the desire in them to accumulate wealth grew, as did a feeling of unhappiness. Being and feeling wealthy is, in some sense, a state of mind. No. I am not philosophising. It truly is. When you are restless about filling your coffers, the less likely you are to enjoy what you *do* have. Start small and simple, and enjoy the process of making that wealth.

List your priorities: What is the first thing you would want if you had the money? Another degree? A car? A comfortable bed? List your wishes by priority. This will help you really understand what you want. Just be honest.

Ensure you are compensated correctly: The first thing to do when you want to attract wealth is to understand where you are with finances. The first step in this exercise would be to ascertain if you are being correctly compensated for the job you do. Some of the research that you can do is:

- Research salary surveys on what people in the same job as you and with similar years of experience get. If you are getting paid lower, consider negotiating a higher salary. This is NOT greed. This is ensuring that you get what you deserve and what you are working for.
- Determine if you are utilising the benefits that your company gives to the fullest. Are you availing all stock options? Travel or gym discounts? 'Ask and ye shall receive', is the saying! Nobody is going to come around reminding you that you should avail all the benefits. It is up to you to do it.

Start looking at your expenses: Much as it can be painstaking and boring, it is really important to keep track of your current finances. Record how much you earn, spend and save. There are several tools available online to help you with this exercise.

Yes, there are rainy days — save!: It is very important to save for a rainy day. Set aside an amount that is sustainable every month. Make sure you allow some room for that occasional pampering. Your past saving techniques may have to be slightly altered to suit your current environment. For instance, saving techniques that worked when you were single may not work now as your priorities have changed.

Find true wealth: As important as it is to save money, it is also good to enjoy the small pleasures that we experience every day. The more you enjoy the simple things, the more you will feel that you are actually saving more! Find joy in meeting up with an old friend, seeing the sun rise, working out at a yoga class … whatever brings you joy will eventually take you to the path of making wealth.

Shloka for abundance and prosperity

Chant this Lakshmi Gayatri mantra to ensure you stay blessed with the required abundance and prosperity and the correct understanding of what it means to have it.

oṁ śrī mahālakṣmyai ca vidmahe
viṣṇu patnyai ca dhīmahi
*tanno lakṣmī pracodayā*t

Meaning

Om. Let us meditate on Mahalakshmi,
The love and consort of Shri Vishnu
May Goddess Lakshmi Devi's radiance inspire our minds and understanding

Devotional songs

The Kanakadhara stotram is a beautiful devotional hymn written by Shri Adi Shankaracharya. Chanting along with M.S. Subbulakshmi's rendition will take you less than nine minutes. Another beautiful hymn from the Rig Vedas on Goddess Mahalakshmi is Shri Suktham, which is a little more difficult to chant, but with a wealth of meaning.

Temples to visit

The Shri Lakshmi Kubera temple in Chennai is the only one dedicated to Lakshmi and Kubera in India.

Legend has it that Kubera, an ardent devotee of Lord Shiva, once performed severe penance to invoke the Lord's blessings. Lord Shiva, being very pleased by Kubera's penance, appeared in front of Kubera along with Goddess Parvati. Apparently Kubera was so taken by the beauty of the Goddess that unknowingly one of his eyes winked. Goddess Parvati was so angered by this that she cursed him and blinded him. Lord Shiva felt pity for his devotee and requested Goddess Parvati to forgive Kubera and restore his eyesight. The Goddess heeded Lord Shiva's request, but only partly. She restored Kubera's eyesight, but made one of his eyes smaller. She also made him the Lord of administering wealth and materials. Since Shri Mahalakshmi is the Goddess for wealth and Lord Kubera is the administrative manager, worshipping both under the same roof will certainly have its benefits.

Harness Your Healing Power

'If you want to see the brave, look at those who can forgive. If you want to see the heroic, look at those who can love in return for hatred.'

– *Bhagavad Gita*

There are two kinds of pain: that which is caused by physical trauma, and the other which has been caused by mental trauma. Physical pain can be controlled to a certain extent with medication. Emotional pain, on the other hand, can be difficult to overcome and it takes a lot of willpower to get back to good mental health.

Very often we are our own worst critic and find it hard to overcome our difficulties as we are constantly living in our past. Our heightened sensitivity to issues and people is because of emotional baggage. The first step to lessening that baggage is to be kinder to yourself. To overcome sadness or stop feeling emotionally dependent, you need to forgive yourself so you can heal.

Anusha is hurt. Her mother is never happy with anything she does, but always seems to say something critical. Anusha feels she's never appreciated. At times, it almost seems that her mother is envious of her. There is a constant war of words between Anusha and her mother. Both of them say things that hurt and that they later regret.

So how do you heal from emotional wounds?

Evaluate the relationship: Take a moment and evaluate the relationship. Is it worth getting upset? There are over seven billion people in the world and if we are allowing one person to hurt us and spoil our day, then that relationship better be worth it. If it is, then you have something special, so all the more reason to calmly talk it out.

Take a walk: Literally! Walking will help calm your nerves and control angry and irrational thoughts, which will help you to see things from the other person's perspective.

Talk only when ready: Once you've calmed down, rehearse in your mind what needs to be said and how to say it.

Do not wait: Don't wait more than a day to mend the relationship. The longer you wait, the harder it is patch things. Waiting also means you will suffer feelings of hurt for longer than you have to.

Shloka 1 for healing oneself

Chanting this healing Rama mantra will help you develop the willpower to fight any emotional and physical pain that comes your way.

oṁ āpadām apahartāram dātāram
sarvasaṁpadām
lokābhirāmam śrīrāmam bhūyo
bhūyo namāmyaham

Meaning

I bow again and again to Shri Rama, who is loved by all, who removes dangers from my path and gives me plenty of wealth.

Shloka 2 for healing oneself

Some situations are beyond our control, no matter how much we plan. It is always nice to take a moment for yourself and chant this shloka. This couplet is from the Vishnu Sahasranamam.

vanamālī gadī ṣār'ngī ṣa'nkhī cakrī ca nandakī
ṣrīmān nārāyaṇo vishṇuh vāsudevo'bhirakshatu

Meaning

The meaning of this shloka can be loosely translated as:
May Lord Narayan who took on the
Auspicious form of Vasudeva, adorned
With the garland of wild flowers
Grant me the protection from all
Sides with the mace,
The bow Sarangi, the conch, the discus, and the sword, Nandaki

Devotional songs

Take some time to memorise the shloka above. After you have memorised it, you might like to listen to

M.S. Subbulakshmi's thirty-minute Vishnu Sahasranamam. It is a chanting of the 1008 names of Maha Vishnu. The names describe beautifully the glorious attributes of the Lord. The full-length version of the very uplifting and healing Apadamapa Hataram shloka sung by T.S. Ranganathan takes less than four minutes to listen to.

Temples to visit

The legend behind the Veeraraghava Swamy Perumal temple in Thiruvallur speaks of complete surrender of oneself and one's problems at the Almighty's feet.

There was once a sage named Salihotra who performed penance for a whole year by fasting and meditating on Lord Vishnu. At the end of his penance, when he was just sitting down to eat, a poor Brahmin knocked on the door asking for food. He gave the Brahmin some of his food. The Brahmin asked for all of the sage's food. Sage Salihotra handed over all the food that he had. After eating, the Brahmin said he was tired and wanted a place to sleep. He asked if he could sleep in the sage's hut, saying 'Evvul (which room) in your abode can I lie down?' From this originated the name of the place, Thiruvallur.

Sage Salihotra offered the Brahmin his home as well. As soon as he gave all that he had, the Brahmin revealed himself to be Lord Vishnu.

The all-merciful deity, known as Vaidhya Veera Raghava Swami, has healing powers to cure any disease or emotional problems.

Nourish Your Body, Mind and Soul

> 'The rhythm of the body, the melody of the mind and the harmony of the soul, create the symphony of life.'
>
> – *B.K.S. Iyengar*

There will be several moments in our lifetimes when we feel undernourished: in our bodies, minds and souls. It could be how you feel when you don't have enough information before making a presentation at a meeting; or not enough food when you are very hungry and you still have an hour to reach home; or your soul isn't ready yet to love somebody after a broken relationship. Having access to nourishment for the body, mind and soul is indeed a blessing.

▯▯

Radha was having a perfectly normal day until she got a call from her child's school. Her daughter, Priyanka, had fallen ill. She rushed to school, picked up the child and went to the doctor. After a battery of tests, it was determined that the child was suffering from a severe eating disorder and was throwing up in school because of it.

Priyanka opened up to her mother that she was living in fear. Fear of putting on weight and not being accepted by her peers. This fear had made the poor child think that she was fat, when she was well within the average weight limit for her age. Her inability to handle social pressure had led her to believe that she was grossly overweight.

Adults also experience this kind of fear and take drastic measures to overcome it instead of looking at it logically.

Talk to the child: Help the child overcome these bouts of anxiety through logical explanations of a balanced diet and exercise, along with prayers. Expose him / her to information about social pressures and eating disorders caused by this. Give your children enough reason to believe in and feel good about themselves.

Help regularise eating habits: Good eating habits, regular meal times and having a working knowledge of healthy food will greatly aid your efforts in helping the child gain a healthy body image, self-worth and self-esteem. It may also require a lifestyle change for the parents as children pick up bad habits from home.

Inform the school authorities: The child spends a significant amount of time in school. The school authorities need to be made aware of the problems that the child is facing, so adequate support can be provided by them. Be mindful of the fact that it is an extremely sensitive topic and needs to be handled with care.

Shloka for nourishment

Chant this shloka to be always blessed with access to nourishment beyond material needs, wisdom and the ability to identify and renounce the small things that don't really matter to your life. It is up to you and the point of time in your life to decide what is important and what is not.

annapūrṇe sadāpūrṇe shaṇkara-prāṇavallabhe
jnāna-vairāgya siddhyarthaṁ bhikṣhāṁ dehi cha Parvati

Meaning

(Oh, Mother Parvati) You are Annapurna, the bestower of food, full of abundance
You are the Lord Shiva's prana
Bless us with the boons of wisdom and renunciation
Bless us though this sacred food

Devotional songs

The Annapurna Ashtakam is a beautiful devotional hymn written by Shri Adi Shankaracharya. M.S. Subbulakshmi brings life to this hymn. It is less than ten minutes. Do listen to it to feel the bliss.

Temples to visit

Hunger related to poverty or ailments vanishes when you pray to Shri Odhavaneswarar, Chottru Thurai Nather, at the Tholaya Selva Nathar temple in Thanjavur, Tamil Nadu. As the name of the Lord indicates, Chottru Durai (Lord of Rice), this temple is where people go to pray for nourishment or alleviation from poverty.

A famine of the worst kind once struck this beautiful village in Thanjavur. Arulalan, an ardent devotee of Lord Shiva, wept and prayed to the Almighty to save the people of the village from hunger and suffering. All of a sudden it began raining incessantly and the entire temple and village was flooded with rainwater. It was dark and wet. The weeping Arulalan suddenly saw something floating towards him. When it came closer to him, he saw that it was a bowl. As soon as he picked it up, he heard a voice saying that it was an 'akshaya pathra' (inexhaustible vessel, in Sanskrit). The voice of the Lord said that the bowl would never be empty and would automatically replenish itself. Arulalan was elated and went on to feed all the people in the village.

Other well-known temples to visit are the Annapurna Devi temple in Varanasi, and the Kamakshi temple in Kanchipuram.

Lead, but with Humility

> 'The beginning of all knowledge comes
> from humility.'
>
> *– Shri Radhanath Swami*

A good leader needs to be knowledgeable and humble. Knowledge is a tool which, if rightly used, can bring a lot of happiness and security. Ignorance may be bliss at certain times to prevent irrational fears and evil thoughts, but it is with the power of knowledge that one can overcome the challenges we face—at the very least through educated guesses!

Knowledge can be acquired in two ways: by educating ourselves, and by observing others. We must understand that the day we cease to learn, we have lost the essence of all the knowledge that we have acquired. And becoming vain about your knowledge is the best way to stop learning.

◻◻

Raghavan was a leader par excellence in a multinational company. His leadership style was very different from the bureaucratic ways his company was used to. The people in his team loved working with him, and the attrition rate dropped drastically. Raghavan understood that intelligence, openness and humility were important characteristics of a good leader, and he followed the rules listed below:

Open door policy: Having an open door policy does not just mean that people are free to enter the boss' cabin. It means keeping an open mind about other people's views and opinions. A good leader always takes the time to listen to what others have to say. Knowledge can only be enhanced by keeping your mind open about inputs from other people. Remember always, the goal is to satisfy your customer, not yourself.

Open to feedback: A humble leader receives negative feedback with self-confidence and positive feedback with poise.

Taking responsibility for actions: A person's reaction to a situation when things don't go too well is a true indicator of how good or bad a leader he / she is. Let's say a product launch does not go off too well. The leader must take responsibility for the situation and must not resort to a blame game, especially in public. If it is indeed the fault of someone in the team, it is best to question him / her separately. This shows that the leader respects everyone equally.

Allowing and helping people to grow: At the beginning of any project, Raghavan called his team members and outlined clearly what his expectations were. He then gave them free rein to accomplish their tasks and had fortnightly meetings with them to discuss their progress. This gave them space to grow in their job, while the progress reports helped him make sure everything was on track.

When the company was going through a massive reorganisation, Raghavan called all those who reported to him and explained the situation. He gave them tips on how they should prepare their résumé, advised them on what kind of roles they would be best in, and assured them that he would give them good recommendations. He spent a significant amount of time coaching and helping these people.

Shloka 1 for knowledge

sarasvati namastubhyaṁ varade kāmarūpiṇi
vidyārambhaṁ kariṣyāmi siddhirbhavatu me sadā

Meaning

This shloka to invoke the blessings of the Goddess of knowledge can be loosely translated as:
Oh, Mother Saraswati, we salute you. You are the giver of many blessings.
Please help us in our efforts to gain knowledge and other noble goals. We depend on you.

Shloka 2 for knowledge

gururbrahmā gururviṣṇurgururdevo maheśvaraḥ
gururdeva paraṁ brahma tasmai śrīgurave namaḥ

Meaning

This shloka invokes the Hindu trinity, and can be loosely translated as:
(The teacher is like) Lord Brahma (who creates this knowledge within us),
Like Lord Vishnu (who steers the knowledge in the right direction within us)

And like Lord Maheshawara (who destroys the wrong concepts attached to our knowledge), while enlightening us on the desired path.
Thus the teacher is like our ultimate God to whom we give our salutations.

Devotional songs

Dakshinamurthy is said to be an incarnation of Lord Shiva, and is a powerhouse for knowledge. The Dakshinamurthy stotram, written by Shri Adi Shankaracharya, takes approximately eleven minutes to chant. The words are in Sanskrit and it takes time and effort to pronounce them well, but its effects on you will make it well worth it. Shankar Mahadevan brings to life the Guru Brahma Guru Vishnu shloka, composed by Shri Kedar Pandit.

Temples to visit

Praying to the deity in the Shri Eyilinathar temple in Salem, Tamil Nadu not only removes obstacles, but also reminds us that however powerful or rich or knowledgeable we may be, humility is required in all our actions.

The legend behind the temple tells the story of how the Pandava Bheema was taught a lesson in humility by Lord Vishnu.

Bheema was very proud of his strength and courage. To teach him a lesson, Lord Vishnu produced a creature known as Purushamirugam, which had a human body and the head of a lion. The creature was so large and ferocious that even Bheema could not stand in front of him. In absolute fear, Bheema kept running away, calling to Krishna for help. He ran through different places — Salem Sukavaneswarar, Uthamachozhapuram Karapuranathar,

Pillur Veeratteswarar, Paramathi Beemeswarar and Nan Sei Idayaru Eyilinathar—performing penances and praying to Lord Shiva for help till finally he learnt his lesson.

Discover the True Power of Information

> 'This is true knowledge: to seek the Self as the true end of wisdom always. To seek anything else is ignorance.'
>
> – *Bhagavad Gita*

When we make mistakes as a child, we are usually easily pardoned with excuses like, 'She is just a child, it's okay', or 'He's just a kid, how could he have known?' As we grow older, the same mistake can be a vacuum that costs lives, causes financial burden and takes away peace. The only way we can prevent situations like this is by ensuring that we're equipped with reliable information. Besides, would it not be better to know that the decision you have made is an informed one?

It was election year in the US. Sanya, originally from a small town in Odisha, was a new immigrant and had minimal knowledge of the world and its affairs. She decided to educate herself with reliable information. After all, this new country was going to be home for a while, and she did not want to be ignorant of the people governing it. Here are some ways she did this.

Do the required research: This research can be on the Internet, books or just by talking to people who understand the information from different points of view.

Ask questions: Do not hesitate to ask people questions. Their answers will only help and not hurt. Never assume that what you are going to ask is a silly question. It never is.

Assimilate your thoughts: After research, it's time to assimilate all your thoughts. If you were gathering information in order to make a decision, go for it now, knowing that whatever action you take is an informed one. Do remember to think of any negative or positive consequences of your action as information too.

Shloka 1 for freedom from ignorance or wrong judgment

This powerful prayer is from the *Upanishads*. Chant this to be blessed with the ability to make the correct decision at defining moments.

oṁ asato mā sadgamaya
tamaso mā jyotirgamaya
mṛtyormā amṛtaṁ gamaya
oṁ śāntiḥ śāntiḥ śāntiḥ

Meaning

Oh Lord, lead me from untruth to truth
From darkness to light,
From death to immortality
Om, peace (in me), peace (in nature), peace (in divine forces)

Devotional songs

Bhaja Govindam is a beautiful hymn composed by Shri Adi Shankaracharya. It challenges our ways and makes us think. M.S. Subbulakshmi brings life to this beautiful hymn. Also listen to the versions of the song 'Asato Ma', in the music album, 'Chants of India' by Ravi Shankar and George Harrison.

Temple to visit

Visit any place of worship that brings you peace and helps you think clearly.

The Sree Swaminathaswami temple, also known as Kumaran Kottam, in Sulur, Coimbatore is the abode of one of the most deeply-loved Gods in south India, Lord Muruga, or Lord Subramanya as He is known in north India.

Lord Muruga is known to have six faces, each with its own significance and serving a specific purpose. One of the faces signifies wisdom, or the removal of ignorance. The Kumaran Kottam is special in that Lord Muruga appears in this temple in separate shrines as He does in the celebrated Aaru Padai Veedu temples, and visiting this temple will give you the immense satisfaction of having visited all six temples.

Educate Yourself; Discover Your Strengths

> 'The wise see knowledge and action as one;
> they see truly.'
>
> – *Bhagavad Gita*

Education is not about adding honorifics to either side of your name. It is not being able to say, 'I am a graduate.' It is more than that.

- It is about discovering your strengths and empowering yourself with information that could be used to conquer great challenges.
- Education is about having the ability to make choices and not be obligated financially to anybody.
- It is insurance for the future. The premium you pay may seemingly be high with the time you spend and effort you make, but the dividends are rich.

Harish was the proverbial child born with a silver spoon in his mouth. He was popular in school and had access to different types of resources to help him exceed academically, but he did not do well in studies. His mind was not on academics. His father ran a very successful business enterprise, and Harish was sure he would inherit it. He had nothing to worry about. He would be rich forever. 'Of what use is education when I already have all that I want?' argued Harish with his dad. His father replied, 'Harish you are a privileged child and I pray to the Almighty that you will always remain so. Do remember that running a business is not child's play. You will need to be educated to make informed decisions in business, as well as in life.' His father went on to say that if a person has been given an opportunity to study, then the following points are very important things to remember:

Have gratitude: You have been given an opportunity to educate yourself. Feel blessed. There are so many children who have not even entered the gates of an educational institution and many others who have done very well for themselves despite access to very little.

Find your passion: Study and educate yourself on topics that interest you. If there is passion, then interest and focus will follow.

Take pride: Give whatever you do your best. Pull out all stops. Make every presentation a work of art, every paper you submit a masterpiece. Give it all you have and the recognition will come on its own.

Have fun: Remember to have fun educating yourself. Education is a lifelong learning process. Find ways to have fun. Get creative!

Shloka 1 to excel in education

oṁ aiṁ mahasarasvathiye namaḥ

Meaning

Om and salutations to Goddess Saraswati, who bestows wisdom.

Shloka 2 to Excel in Education

jñānānanda mayaṁ devaṁ
nirmalam sphaṭikākṛtiṁ
ādhāraṁ sarvavidyānaṁ hayagrīvaṁ upāsmahe

Meaning

We meditate upon Lord Hayagriva, who is the personification of knowledge and bliss, whose form is like a flawless crystal and who is the basis of all branches of learning.

Devotional songs

The Saraswati Vandana shloka, 'Ya kundendu tushara haradhavala', is an endearing shloka. The version sung by Shri Unni Krishnan takes under four minutes to chant. Prema Rengarajan's CD, 'Listen and Learn: Prayers for Kids', includes the Shri Hayagriva Stuti, and it is very easy to memorise.

Temples to visit

The ancient temple of Gnana Saraswathi at Basara, situated near Hyderabad, is said to have exceptional powers. It is the abode not only of Goddess Saraswati but also of Goddess Kali and Goddess Lakshmi.

Build Self-Esteem; Grow Positive

'Neither in this world nor elsewhere is there any happiness in store for him who always doubts.'

– Bhagavad Gita

Intelligence alone is not enough. You need self-confidence and communication skills for it to manifest benefits. Self-confidence allows you to overcome the most difficult of challenges. It is nothing but a state of accepting who you are. It is at once your greatest tool for doing good and also your greatest defence against harm.

Aishu used to feel tired all the time. Her health was normal; she was an active person and she ate well. Yet, the feeling of tiredness persisted. She consulted a general physician who was also a close friend. When Aishu explained her problem, Dr Geetha — who was familiar with Aishu's family situation — realised that Aishu was on the brink of depression. Dr Geetha could see that, subconsciously, Aishu was hurt by many issues but did not have the self-esteem to voice her opinion. She needed help.

The most challenging part about maintaining self-esteem is when there is constant exposure to negative people who can never see or maybe who never *want* to see others overcome challenges and do well. They slowly take away all the positive feeling that we may have developed within ourselves. It is very easy to get sucked into this quagmire.

Do not let that happen to you.

Your immediate surroundings matter: Surround yourself with positive people who add value to your everyday life. Your life partner, your children and your friends are the most important part of you. You cannot choose your family, but you can certainly ensure that you choose your life partner and friends well. Being around them should boost your confidence.

Do not cater to other people's tastes: Author and fashion consultant Tim Gunn says, 'You have no control over other people's taste, so focus on staying true to your own.' Doesn't this make sense? Very often we get pulled into catering to other people's tastes and standards, even if it does not suit ours, just to feel accepted and gain approval. This is a sure path to the destruction of confidence.

Give selective permission: As former First Lady of the United States Eleanor Roosevelt said, 'No one can make you feel inferior without your consent.' People hurt others because they are hurting inside. It is very hard to take such a philosophical stand, though, when people take all kinds of efforts to hurt you. The best thing to do would be to move away from the person and situation. This way you are not allowing him / her to be part of your life and the ability to hurt you any more.

Trust yourself: One of the biggest enemies of your self-confidence is yourself. Do you constantly hear a little voice telling you: you are not beautiful, you are not strong; you are not smart? That voice is you. The only role that other people play is in encouraging that voice. Create an inner self that you will be happy with for life.

Learn to draw boundaries and say 'no': Learning to say 'no' is an art. Saying 'no' comes easy to people when they are not dependent on others to boost their self-esteem. People who are dependent on others for praise, or who feel obligated (emotionally or financially), find it very difficult to say 'no' and establish clear boundaries. Learning this art, along with a fair touch of diplomacy, will ensure that hurt and expectations stay far away from you.

In author and scholar Brene Brown's words, 'Talk to yourself like you would to someone you love.'

Shloka for building self-confidence

The Hanuman mantra is sure to build your self-confidence.

manojavaṁ mārutatulyavegaṁ
jitendriyaṁ buddhimatāṁ variṣṭhaṁ
vātātmajaṁ vānarayūthamukhyaṁ
śrīrāmadūtaṁ śaraṇaṁ prapadye

Meaning

I take refuge in Shri Hanuman, who is as swift as the mind and fast as wind,
Who is the master of the senses and honoured for His wisdom,

Who is the son of the Wind God and chief among the Monkeys,
To that messenger of Shri Rama, I take refuge.

Devotional songs

The Hanuman Ashtothram is a truly uplifting chanting of the 1008 names of Lord Hanuman. Just the act of concentrating on the difficult words and pronunciation is enough to strengthen your mind.

Temples to visit

Lord Hanuman is described as one who is an embodiment of fearlessness and self-confidence. With a can-do attitude, success is a natural outcome. In the Shri Jayaveera Abhayahastha Anjaneya temple in Krishnapuram (near Tirunelveli), the deity is majestic and about six feet tall. The right hand of the deity is in abhaya mudra, which means He protects all His devotees from fear.

The Madhya Kailash temple in Chennai has become famous for its unique idol. The Adhyantha Prabhu deity is half-Ganesha and half-Hanuman. The idol was crafted after a vision of such a form was seen by one of the temple officials.

Healthy Days Beget Happy Zzzs

> *'Long is the night for the sleepless, long is the league for the weary one; samsara's (cycle of existence) way is long for fools who know not the Dhamma True.'*
>
> – Gautama Buddha

Sleeplessness, or insomnia, is a real problem that exists nowadays. The inability to sleep could come from a variety of issues caused by physical, mental or emotional problems affecting the body. Good sleep is considered a form of meditation and is extremely important for the body to regain its energy lost during the day. This vicious cycle of sleep deprivation and energy loss has to be curbed somewhere, and the best time to start is now and the best place to start is in your own head.

Sanyuktha, a busy executive in her forties, suffered from insomnia. She was trying to balance a busy home life and work-related pressures. The lack of family support did not help her condition in any way and she was becoming increasingly stressed, leading to more nights without sleep. She decided to enrol herself in a yoga and meditation class. Six months later, she found amazing results in her sleep patterns. Here are some things she learned on her journey to overcoming sleeplessness.

Sow the right grain: The type of food you consume at night plays an important role in the inability to fall asleep at night. Consuming foods high in carbohydrates, salt or oil, or desserts rich in sugar and cream, or large amounts of alcohol, can all trigger insomnia. It is a good practice to eat at least three hours prior to going to bed. Consume foods that are light on the stomach and easy to digest. If you are hungry, bananas are a good fruit to consume an hour before bedtime. A nightcap made of milk, turmeric, honey and saffron will help calm the mind before you hit the sack. Do remember to brush your teeth, though!

Stick to the same routine: Sleeping and waking up at the same time every day helps the body to adjust to a particular rhythm. Frequent travellers will need to find ways to adjust their sleep pattern in a way that suits them, as each body is different.

Stock up on water during the day: When the body is dehydrated, the legs sometimes experience cramps or muscle spasms at night. Stretching the leg can help relieve the pain, but it also wakes you up from your sleep. To prevent this from happening, ensure you consume enough water during the day. Restrict the amount you drink an hour before you go to bed, to decrease the need to go to the bathroom in the middle of the night.

Siesta time must be shortened: While recent studies show that taking a short nap in the middle of the day helps increase one's efficiency, it is also important not to sleep for too long. The idea is to teach the body to adhere to a specific wake and sleep pattern; sleeping too much in the afternoon, will disrupt that pattern.

Seasonal change adaptation: If you are living in a place that becomes dark very quickly, then ensure that your home is well lit inside. Draw the curtains open in your bedroom so sunlight can enter in the morning.

Set the stage: The place where you sleep has to be your bedroom. If you tend to fall asleep on the couch while watching TV, you should stop the habit immediately. The bedroom must be clean, airy and devoid of clutter. The bed sheets must be changed at least once in fifteen days. The temperature in the room must be set at a level that is optimum for sleep, if you are using air-conditioning.

Suspend use of technology: Say a strict 'No' to using phones, tablets and watching TV before going to bed. Instead read a book that calms your mind or listen to calming instrumental music before you go to sleep. One of the best ways to stay away from the phone is to charge it outside your bedroom. Ask people to call you on the landline for emergencies. Give your mind a break.

Say your prayers: Get into a habit of saying a prayer every morning. Learning to chant shlokas engages the mind in a practice that helps relieve stress.

Strengthen your muscles: Half an hour of exercise every day is a must. Walking, running, or any exercise that pumps up your adrenaline levels will lead to a good night's sleep.

Soothe and clean your body: Practise the habit of having a bath before you retire for the day. Ensure that your feet are washed, dried and moisturised well before you get to bed. Change into loose-fitting clothing that is washed well and does not smell. This simple habit will make you feel free of discomfort.

Spirit of breathing: Sleeplessness is a state of restlessness in the mind caused by a disturbed bio-rhythm. This obviously needs to be set right. Apart from adhering to the tips above, simple breathing practices must be learnt and practised. One particular form of breathing practice in yoga is known as Bramhari Pranayama or the humming bee breath. This helps to shut the world off from your thoughts.

Note: Please ensure that you learn how to use this practice from a certified yoga instructor.

1. Sit down in sukhasana, your spine erect. If it helps, sit on a cushion.
2. Raise your arms to the level of your ears.
3. Cover your ears with your thumbs.
4. Place the two index fingers above your forehead.
5. Place the two middle fingers over your closed eyes.
6. The little fingers should be placed gently on the sides of your nostrils. All the external noise will now be completely shut off.
7. Inhale and fill your lungs with air.
8. Exhale and push all the inhaled air out slowly, while keeping your mouth closed.
9. As you exhale, make a humming sound like that of a bee. The sound should be continuous and as loud as you can make it.

This humming sound will cause vibrations in your head and make you feel calm and peaceful with repeated practice. Ensure that your eyes and mouth are always closed throughout the entire practice. Try and practise this breathing technique throughout the day to help calm your mind.

Shloka to cure sleeplessness

The simplest of mantras to cure sleeplessness is the Pranava mantra or simply the word 'Om'. Om is the combination of 'Aaa' + 'Ooo' + 'Mmm'. The Pranava mantra is the primordial sound from which the whole spiritual universe was created. The word Om can be chanted in many ways, but chanting as follows helps to calm the mind and focus on the chanting better:

1. Start by taking a deep breath and chant Om softly, focusing on the 'O' of the word. For example: 'Ooooooooooooooommm'.
2. Take a deep breath and then chant Om softly, focusing on the 'M' of the word. For example: 'Ommmmmmmmmmm'.
3. Imagine the sound of the mantra in your mind and chant internally, 'Oooooommm'.
4. Repeat this throughout the day as many times as you can. Try using this mantra every time you are feeling perturbed or anxious.

Meaning

The different religions that embrace this mantra provide different meanings for this word. One definition is that the word Om represents God himself and the soul (atman) within you. Chanting the mantra is bound to bring you closer to the divine.

Devotional songs

In the ancient text *Devi Mahatmyam* (Durga Saptashati), written by Sage Markandeya in praise of the divine Goddess Durga, there are four main hymns. One of them, the Brahma Stuthi, also known as the Tantrokta Ratri Suktam, is sung in praise of Devi Durga. This particular hymn is known to resolve issues pertaining to insomnia. The version sung by Anuradha Paudwal takes less than four minutes to chant.

Legend has it that Lord Brahma was being bothered by two demons and prayed to Lord Vishnu for help. At that time, Lord Vishnu was in Yoga Nidra (the state of deep sleep yet remaining awake) and he could not be woken up. Lord Brahma then invoked the blessings of Nidra Devi, the Goddess of sleep, to awaken Lord Vishnu. Nidra Devi obliged and Lord Vishnu awoke from his deep slumber to save the Universe from the misery of the demons.

Temple to visit

Any temple would bring the desired peace and calmness in your mind to set right your sleep patterns. Until such time as your body gets into a perfect rhythm, it is recommended that you find peace and solace within your home. After you do, plan a visit to temples or places of worship that allow you to follow your daily routine and physical comfort requirements, while offering your thanks to the Lord.

Allow Not the (Evil) Eye to Fool the Mind

'The man who foolishly does me wrong, I will return to him the protection of my most ungrudging love; and the more evil comes from him, the more good shall go from me.'

– Gautama Buddha

The world that we live in now is increasingly competitive. Competition is good as long as it is healthy. Unfortunately, there are people who feel the need to compete with others, irrespective of their age or where they belong. Greed and envy seem to be the basis of different types of hatred. In most religions, there are a lot of stories about the evil eye and the bad effects it has on others. Of course, in this modern-day world, the younger generation would probably laugh and say there is no such thing as the evil eye and mark it down under superstition. The 'evil eye', to give it a more befitting modern-day definition, is nothing but bad vibes — an emotion wrought with bad thoughts and evil intentions. Sometimes we feel good in certain people's presence and sometimes we don't — this discomfort can be attributed to these very vibes being sent out.

◻◻

Shanthi is a young girl in her thirties. She is married and well accomplished with a successful career. She manages the delicate balance of her home and office very efficiently and has worked very hard to achieve that balance. Priya, her colleague at work, struggles to achieve that balance and cannot handle Shanthi's success. Every time Shanthi says something about her achievements or that of her family's, Priya burns with an inner envious rage, but portrays a very sweet demeanour to Shanthi. Shanthi is getting increasingly uncomfortable in Priya's presence and has decided not to share any of her accomplishments with her, but how can she prevent Priya's envy from hurting her and her family? What should she do?

Recognise the difference: Some emotional intelligence is required here. You need to be able to recognise the difference between a one-off situation and a continuously negative reaction to your successes. If the bad vibes continue, then take the necessary action. Do understand that everybody goes through ups and downs in their lives. It may well be that the person has just had a rough day and wasn't in the mood to hear about someone else's success. Of course, it does not warrant bad behaviour from them, but recognise that this could be a passing phase. You need people around you and cannot keep eliminating each and everyone because of one reaction.

Move away: There is really nothing you can do if somebody did not feel happy about your successes. They are creating their own karma. You need to move on and move away from the person who does not make you feel good about yourself. You do not deserve that treatment.

Surround yourself with goodness: To feel good about yourself, you need to recognise that you do not need validation from anyone, not even your mother. To feel happy, you only need one person — yourself. Of course, sharing one's happiness feels good, but share it only with people who care. Surround yourself with people who genuinely care for you and your happiness. If you cannot find anyone at that particular point of time, then find a charity to share your happiness. Volunteer for a day with a charity and you will find that the joy and gratitude that the less privileged give is a lot more than what you have given.

Shloka to ward off evil

Chant the Pratyangira Gayatri mantra to feel peaceful that the Almighty is taking care of all bad thoughts that come your way.

ŏm āparajeethaya vidmahe
Pratyangiraya dhīmahi
ṭhano ūgra pracotayāt
ŏm Pratayangiraya vidmahe
ṣathrunisoothiniya dhīmahi
ṭhano ḍevi Prajothayāth

Meaning

Om, Om, Let us meditate on the Goddess who cannot be conquered,
Let us meditate on Goddess Pratyangira
Let her fierce form inspire our minds,

Let us meditate on Goddess Pratyangira,
Let us meditate on the one who kills enemies,
Let the Goddess illuminate our minds.

Devotional songs

The Mahishaduramardhini stotram written by Shri Adi Shankaracharya is a beautiful hymn praising Goddess Kali, who killed the demon Mahishasura. The Mahishasuramardhini stotram sung by the Bombay Sisters takes less than eighteen minutes to chant. Listen to this hymn to feel uplifted.

The Kandar Sashti Kavacham, sung by the Sulamangalam sisters, takes less than twenty minutes to chant. It is a beautiful hymn composed by Devaraya Swamigal, a researcher. This hymn talks of how each part of the body and mind is protected by the Almighty. Listen to this hymn to feel well-protected by a higher power, always.

Temples to visit

Visit the Pratyangira temple in Sholinganallur, near Chennai, to get rid of the anxiety caused by the fear of evil thoughts from others. Artharvana Bhadra Kali, as the Goddess is also called, is an avatar of Goddess Parvati. Pratyangira Devi is known to protect Dharma or the righteous path. Legend has it that in the war between Rama and Ravana, Ravana lost all his sons except Indrajit. Indrajit was known for his war crafts and had the ability to defeat even Lord Indra. It is believed that Indrajit decided to perform the Nikumbala Yajna to invoke the blessings of Atharvana Kali and gain knowledge of all the wizardry of the tantras and mantras. Lord Rama learnt of this and prevented the completion of the yajna by performing pujas to the Goddess himself. Apparently Goddess Pratyangira, who is known to be very fair and just, blessed Lord Rama with infinite power and strength to overthrow Ravana and his son Indrajit, and to rescue Devi Sita from Lanka. She blessed Rama with this power as she knew that Lord Rama's intentions were pure, good and just, whereas those of Indrajit were unjust and evil.

Temples such as Gunaseelam in Tiruchi, Tamil Nadu, Chottanikkara Bhagavati temple in Kerala, and Tiruvidaimaruthur in Tanjore, Tamil Nadu, are known to help people overcome the ill effects of envy and hence fear.

The Golden Years of Life

> 'It is said, if you want to know what you were doing in the past ... look at your body now. If you want to know what will happen to you in the future ... look at what your mind is doing now.'
>
> – *The Dalai Lama*

Often, by the time people reach retirement, they are worn out, mentally, emotionally and physically. In order to feel at peace with oneself, it is best to cut down the things that you have to monitor and oversee. In your old age you have less physical stamina and constrained finances, so it becomes a challenge just to go about normal routines during the day, let alone having to think of God and evolution. When I say cut down on responsibilities, I mean by starting with simple things. Develop the will and courage to downsize your home and minimise the material things that you will need to take care of. The more you have, the more you need to take care of. Let go of the unnecessary, one by one. Harmony and peace begins with the way you keep your home. De-cluttering your home helps to de-clutter your mind. This is the essence of Feng Shui and Vaastu Shastra.

Mr and Mrs Devdutt were in their late seventies and lived in India by themselves. They had two daughters, both of whom lived abroad with their families. Mr and Mrs Devdutt led a fairly peaceful retired life. They had planned their finances well for their retirement and now lived very self-sufficiently. One day their neighbour Swetha visited them. They were having a lovely long conversation. A joke was made by Swetha and both Mr and Mrs Devdutt started laughing, all the time holding each other's hands. At that instant Swetha was struck by the simplicity of their home, their lives and the happiness that surrounded all of that. 'How is it that you both look so happy all the time, Aunty and Uncle? How does your home look so clean always? How do you manage so well all by yourselves? Please share the secret with Adith and me. We are half your age and already feel so overwhelmed.'

The couple smiled at Swetha. Mr Devdutt stroked the palm of his wife's hand gently and said, 'You know Swetha, I am a lucky man. This beautiful lady here has magical hands and whatever they touch does not become gold, but definitely is worth treasuring. This is not rocket science as they say, my dear child, but simple planning; planning in advance to retire from worldly pleasures.'

Swetha looked at both of them, puzzled and curious, and asked, 'How do we learn to renounce worldly pleasures when the need for physical comfort only increases with age?'

'True, my dear, very true,' Mrs Devdutt said. 'Let me elaborate on the generous compliment that my dear handsome husband just gave me.'

Plan your finances well: Planning your finances is the key to any mental happiness and peace. You definitely do not want to be saddled with financial pressures when the earning power has decreased and expenses only increase. Save well and enough for a life where your needs are met.

Let it go, gracefully: Start decluttering your home, when your children leave the nest. It is the best time to start. For example, make a single photo collage of your favourite photographs and hang it up. Put the rest in boxes and give them away to people who would cherish them. This way you don't have stacks of albums to take care of. We are capable of attaching sentiment to the smallest safety pin. Remember that memories are created in your mind. You do not need a material object to enjoy thinking about it. Let go. It is just a pin. Let go. It is just a plastic box. Let go, because it's okay to let go.

Make determined changes: Other small changes that can dramatically help are:

- Prepare a menu for the week.
- Eat every two hours. Include fruits, vegetables and nuts, depending on your health requirements.
- Exercise morning and evening; at least go for short walks.
- Engage with young kids, it'll keep you thinking and make you happy.

You should have only one aim: to live happily.

Shloka to help realise God's presence

This is the first shloka from the *Ishavasya Upanishad.*

oṁ īśā vāsyamidaṁ sarvaṁ yatkiñca jagatyāṁ jagat
tena tyaktena bhuñjīthā mā gṛdhaḥ kasyasviddhanam

Meaning

The entire Universe is enveloped and covered by the Supreme Being
Whatever is apparently moving or not moving, all that is Ishvara.
Knowing this, be happy without the sense of possessiveness with regard to any object

Devotional songs

Listen and chant along with the Namo Ratna Trayaya on Lord Avalakotiswara, the Buddhist lord of compassion. This is sure to levitate you to different heights and help revive the compassion in you.

Ani Choying Drolma is a Nepalese Buddhist nun and musician from the Nagi Gompa monastery in Nepal, who is known for the music composition of Tibetan Buddhist chants. The music composed by her for this mantra takes under five minutes to follow and chant.

Temples to visit

The Thillai Natrajar temple in Chidambaram is a must-see. It is the abode of Lord Shiva and Parvati. This temple is most popularly known for something called 'Chidambara Rahasyam'. Translated from Tamil, it means, 'The secret of Chidambaram'.

In a small room, behind a curtain, close to the main deity, is the 'secret'. The secret is the Akasha Linga, or the powers of the Lord, embedded in a yantra or amulet which has geometric designs representing cosmic energies. This Akasha Linga represents one of the five elements of nature — akaasam (space).

The rahasyam, or secret, has a deep philosophical meaning associated to it. In essence, it means you do not need a form to pray to, or an object to hold, to feel the existence of God. God is present in all that you do; God is around you and with you, always.

Shlokas to Improve Physical Health

Physical health is the best kind of wealth that one can accumulate when young. This is often overlooked until ill health strikes you. A good diet and an active lifestyle that suits your needs and maintains fitness will establish your first line of defence against illness. Complete wellbeing comes from being physically and mentally well and using this to the best of our abilities to practise gratitude.

Know your comfort zone: Physical wellbeing is relative. We need to constantly remind ourselves that we are not in a race. What makes us comfortable physically could be very different from what makes another person comfortable. According to Patanjali's *Yoga Sutras*, verse II-46, 'Sthiram Sukham Asanam' means any asana when practised should be stable, and make you happy and comfortable. If the asana is causing you discomfort of any kind, then you are doing something that does not suit your body. This verse can be extended to even our day-to-day living. Understanding one's own comfort zone is very important. Physical ailments could be linked to non-adherence to one's own comfort zone for an extended period of time. One's performance is directly related to the comfort zone. The higher the level of mental, physical and emotional comfort, the better is the performance.

Carve out your comfort zone: It is up to us to vocalise our needs, without sounding apologetic. The type of food we eat, the time when we eat it, the way in which it is prepared could all be very different from what another person is used to. Now, putting up with discomfort when you are on vacation or staying with somebody else for a short while is one thing, but do make sure that you do not make a lifetime of sacrificing your comforts. Understanding your body's needs and addressing it is important. By that,

I don't mean obsessing over one's needs, but recognising the minimal that is required so your body does not send you reminders. These reminders come in the form of physical and emotional ailments. Do also bear in mind that these comfort zones keep changing based on your lifestyle changes as well your age. Tune in to these changes and address them.

Balance the different zones: Realistic challenges to address the needs of all at home especially when you are the sole bread winner or are the caregiver can be quite daunting and extremely tiring. This is when you need to seek spiritual guidance and peace through prayers and chants. These chants will give you the much needed 'me time' and allow you to bring creative options and ideas to overcome these challenges. It might just boil down to spending more money, but remember there are no free lunches! Everything has a cost, and so does physical comfort. Feel blessed that you have the ability to recognise the cause and are able to arrive at a solution. Do not make the solution itself a problem!

The next few chapters walk you through some common physical ailments and steps that could be taken to prevent/ minimise the pain and help relieve you of the condition over a period of time. Wishes in plenty for a healthy life!

Heal Your Body

> 'Man surprised me most about humanity. Because he sacrifices his health in order to make money. Then he sacrifices money to recuperate his health. And then he is so anxious about the future that he does not enjoy the present; the result being that he does not live in the present or the future; he lives as if he is never going to die, and then dies having never really lived.'
>
> – *The Dalai Lama*

Harness the positive energy in yourself, eat well and stay fit to ensure that you are healthy throughout your life. Here are some things you can do to kickstart better health.

General tips

Lifestyle: Adopt a lifestyle that suits your personality, physical abilities and resources. It is good to have ambitions, but make sure they match your lifestyle and family — there's no point in having goals that don't align with these. Any disconnect here is bound to cause frustration and disillusionment. Very often physical problems occur when there is abuse to the body and mind over a long period of time. When we are younger, we push the boundaries of our physical and mental capacities. This takes a toll on us when we least expect it. It is extremely important to draw boundaries. To do that, it starts by simply saying a 'No', to others and to ourselves.

Follow a good diet: In this increasingly hectic and fast-paced life, it is getting difficult to follow a good diet though it plays an integral role in our physical wellbeing. Make the time to prepare some easy, healthy recipes so you can eat food that is nourishing and fresh.

There is a lot of information on the Internet now on nutrition and diets. There are different types of diets out there, but one must take care to choose a diet that suits your lifestyle and pocket. Care must be taken to ensure that the four food groups are incorporated in the daily diet. The four food groups being:

- Cereals, millets and pulses
- Vegetables and fruits
- Milk and milk products, egg, meat and fish
- Oils and fats and nuts and oilseeds

According to the National Institute of Nutrition in India, a balanced diet is one where 50–60 per cent of total calories come from complex carbohydrates, about 10–15 per cent from proteins and 20–30 per cent from fat. First, to make eating the right foods more interesting and easy, you really do need to ensure that diet and cooking is organised. Here are some tips to ensure cooking and eating do not become arduous tasks:

- Plan a whole week's menu ahead of time, during the weekend. This will ensure that you do the required shopping for the vegetables and other groceries.

- If you're short on time, find grocery stores that sell pre-cut vegetables and fruits.
- Organise the foods in the fridge according to their expiration date.
- If you are lucky enough and live in a place where there are no power-cuts, prepare some gravies and put it into the freezer.
- Wash, dry and store vegetables like tomatoes, herbs such as curry leaves and coriander leaves, ginger and green chillies in airtight containers. This becomes easier to take out as and when needed.
- Always wash and then cut the vegetables or fruits. This prevents leaching of essential vitamins such as vitamin B and C from the vegetables or fruits.
- Do not throw out the water in which you cook vegetables. This water has essential minerals and vitamins. To begin with, cook vegetables in as little water as possible. Use the water later to liquefy a gravy, or cool it down and add to curd to make buttermilk. If the vegetables can be steamed, that would be best. (Note: there are vegetables like yam that will cause itching in the throat if the water in which it is cooked is consumed.)
- Meat products are good for health, but only when eaten moderately. Ensure that you adhere to the shelf life and expiration date on the meat products to avoid food poisoning. Eggs and milk products are also to be consumed in moderation in accordance with the daily allowances and requirements of your lifestyle.
- Yoghurt is very good for health — there is a reason your grandma probably insisted you eat it. It has

natural probiotics in it and helps to set right the stomach's digestive system. Get creative and either buy or make fruit yoghurt, so there is an incentive for you to have the yoghurt, in case you do not like the taste.

- Do some research on supposedly taboo foods. For instance, ghee (clarified butter) which is homemade is actually very good for the body. It is known as 'annam shudhi' or that which cleans the food. Moderation is the key to any food consumed. A teaspoon of ghee along with your rice or roti will help your system immensely.

Some general diet tips are given below. Follow these unless you have some very specific diet restrictions:

- ***Breaking the fast***: Have breakfast or at least a fruit before your coffee or tea in the morning. The stomach is left empty for an average of seven to eight hours overnight and eating something first is extremely important to 'break the fast'. Start your day with a tall glass of tepid water and a banana. This helps to prepare the stomach better for the coffee or tea that you might take later on.
- ***Break the habit***: Avoid coffee or tea if possible. Coffee or tea hinders the absorption of certain essential minerals and vitamins in the body, thus slowing down the process of healing. If you are already addicted to either of these caffeinated drinks, then decrease the amount consumed.
- ***Breakfast like a king***: Start your day with a good breakfast; this is imperative in any balanced diet. Do not skip breakfast and avoid eating it while

commuting. It is imperative that you make time to have a wholesome meal before you leave for work.

- ***Filler foods***: Have small frequent meals through the day. If you have breakfast around 8 a.m., ensure that you have something to eat by 10.30 a.m. Have these filler foods again after your lunch and before dinner. These filler foods help to cut down the acidity in the stomach. The more frequently you eat, the better it is for the body. Some of the types of foods that you can have are clear soups, buttermilk, fruits, dry fruits and nuts, sundal (a south Indian preparation of steamed lentils). Smoothies made of oats, honey, almond powder, fruits and yoghurt serve as good fillers and are extremely nutritious as well. Quantity is the key. Cut down on quantities but increase the frequency.
- ***Lunch like a commoner***: Load up your plate with high-fibre vegetables. This will cut down the amount of other foods you eat, such as rice.
- ***Dinner like a pauper***: Dinner has to be lighter than lunch and the amount of carbohydrates consumed during dinner should be preferably less than that eaten at lunch. For this, fill up your stomach first with vegetables.
- ***Hydrate, hydrate, hydrate***: Drink at least eight to ten glasses of water every day. This helps to flush out all the toxins in the body and keeps the body hydrated. One of the best ways to ensure this is done is to measure out ten glasses of water in a bottle. Ensure you finish the bottle by the end of the day so you do not have to keep count of the glasses of water you have consumed.

- ***Eat slowly***: The longer you take to chew, the better it is. It takes almost twenty minutes for the stomach to realise it is full. Slowing down while eating and enjoying the meal ensures that the signal that the stomach is giving is recognised immediately.

Exercise: Any kind of exercise will improve your health, but yoga combines especially well with a chanting routine. It is highly recommended that you start learning and practising yoga with a good yoga teacher. When done properly, yoga is thought to benefit every organ in the body. At the very least, it gets you moving!

Shloka to heal the body

Chant the Maha Mrityunjaya shloka (also called Rudra mantra) every day to ensure that you and your family are blessed with good health throughout your lives.

oṁ tryambakaṁ yajāmahe
sugandhiṁ puṣṭivardhanam
urvārukamiva bandhanān
mṛtyormukṣīya māmṛtāt

Meaning

We meditate on the Three-eyed reality,
That which permeates and nourishes all like a fragrance.
May we be liberated from death for the sake of immortality,
Even as the cucumber is severed from bondage to the creeper.

Devotional songs

The Dhanavantri Maha Mantra Japam sung by T.S. Ranganathan takes less than twenty-five minutes to chant and is extremely uplifting. Lord Dhanavantri is the

Lord of medicine for healing, and this hymn is in praise of him.

Yoga asanas for general good health

The asanas prescribed here are in accordance with the teachings of renowned yoga practitioners. The following asanas boost immunity, hence lead to good health.

Note: Please perform these asanas only after consulting with your physician.

Learn the asanas from a learned yoga practitioner.

- Uttanasana
- Adho mukha svanasana
- Prasarita padottanasana
- Sirsasana
- Viparita dandasana
- Sarvangasana
- Halasana
- Setu bandha sarvangasana
- Viparita karani
- Savasana

Temples to visit

The presiding deity at the Marundeeswarar temple in Chennai is Lord Shiva in the form of Marundeeswarar. It is believed that praying at this temple will cure people of diseases and health ailments.

According to legend, there were once two evil demon brothers named Vatapi and Ilvala. They came up with a plan to kill sages: Vatapi would turn into a goat and be served to them. When the time was right, Ilvala would call out to him and chant a mantra that would bring his brother back alive. Vatapi would then tear open the stomach of the sage and come out. This plan, however, did not work on Sage Agastya as he digested Vatapi before he could come out.

Digesting Vatapi gave Sage Agastya a lot of pain in his stomach. To cure him, Lord Shiva made a herbal medicine and gave it to him. Agastya then learnt the cures for all types of diseases from Lord Shiva at this temple. 'Marunthu' in Tamil means medicine, hence the name Marundeeswarar for Lord Shiva.

There is also the Jwarahareswarar temple in Kanchipuram; devotees believe that visiting the temple cures people of frequent reoccurrences of unexplained fever.

Heal Your Wounds

> 'Our sorrows and wounds are healed only when we touch them with compassion.'
>
> – *Gautama Buddha*

When recovering from an ailment or surgery, doctors and the people caring for you can only help you with medicines and soothing words. To overcome it faster, it is important that you remain positive and will yourself to heal.

General tips to heal quicker

Surrender yourself completely to the power of the Almighty and your positive intentions. Take charge of the situation and do not give in to self-pity. Self-pity will drain you *and* everyone else around you.

- Focus on one task at a time. Don't multitask especially when you are sick.
- Ask for help. The worst thing to do is to tolerate pain beyond measure or self-medicate. There are medical professionals to determine if pain

or any wound needs intervention. Leave it to the professionals to make that call.

- Stay well hydrated (unless the doctor has advised limited fluid intake).
- Get extra help for chores if you can.
- Remain positive. Some tips to do so:
    - o Listen to soothing music.
    - o Keep away from people you do not get good vibes from. Some people are just toxic for you and your system
    - o Try and stay away from smart phones and Internet before going to bed. Do not read about your symptoms or illness online — it will only make you worry more. Read a book that inspires you instead.
    - o Do not feel the need to immediately respond to every message or email that comes your way. Make use of technology and send automated messages; this will alleviate their concern about your health and assure them that you will get back to them soon.
- Ensure that the kitchen is well-stocked with vitamin- and mineral-rich foods that help you heal faster.
    - o Vitamin A helps in the growth of epithelial cells, which cover the external and internal surface of the body. Foods rich in vitamin A, such as carrot, yellow squash, sweet potato, mango, and dark green leafy vegetables such as kale or spinach, help in the growth of these epithelial cells.
    - o Vitamin B and C are water-soluble vitamins. What this essentially means is that you need to

replenish the body with these vitamins every day. Vitamin B is important in the healing process by helping to break down the proteins and carbohydrates necessary to heal wounds. Most B vitamins are found in legumes and plant-based foods, although the primary source for vitamin B12 is meat, eggs and dairy. If you are a vegan or a strict vegetarian, speak to your doctor about getting vitamin B12 supplements.

- Vitamin C plays an important role in regulating immune system deficiencies. It plays a very important role in the healing process by providing new scar tissue. Fruits rich in vitamin C are the citrus fruits, gooseberry, cauliflower, tomatoes and papayas.
- Zinc helps to build the immune system. Foods rich in zinc are pumpkin seeds, shrimp and broccoli.

You can use the following foods found commonly in Indian cuisine as part of your diet, but consult with your doctor before you use any of it on an open wound.

- Ginger: This root found in abundance in India, is a very good pain-killer and is known to have analgesic properties. One of the popular methods to treat pain in the olden days was to apply dried ginger (sukku) packs on swollen areas. Dried ginger powder is also very effective in healing sinus-related headaches, as it helps to absorb the water retention that causes this pain.
- Turmeric: The antioxidant property of turmeric is known to heal wounds. Add a pinch of turmeric and pepper to hot milk at night and consume

before sleeping. This calms the stomach and heals wounds faster.

- o Cinnamon: This spice is loaded with antioxidants that help in the healing of wounds. There is documented evidence to prove that it helps to regulate blood sugar levels too.
- o Honey: Honey is known to have antibacterial and anti-inflammatory properties. If you have a throat ache, consuming a paste made of one teaspoon of honey and cinnamon will help it.

Shloka 1 to heal wounds

The phrase provided here is essentially auto-suggestion — you tell yourself you are healing and so, in fact, feel better as you do.

aham ārogyaṁ

Meaning

The phrase means, 'I am healthy!', and works like an affirmation.

Shloka 2 to heal wounds

The Buddhist Goddess White Tara (Sita Tara) is associated with healing, good health and long life. She is known for her power to heal swiftly. The White Tara mantra is the root Tara mantra followed by additional words of affirmation used to heal quicker. It is a strong request made to the Goddess for increased life, an ethical lifestyle and wisdom.

oṁ tāre tuttāre ture svāḥ,
mama Ayuḥ punya Jñānā puṣtiṃ kuru svāh

Meaning

The approximate translation of this shloka is: I prostrate to the Liberator, Mother of all the Victorious Ones to liberate me from samsara, disease and fears and give me an increasingly ethical life filled with wisdom and merit.

This mantra can be changed from a generalised prayer to positive affirmation for a specific person. For example, if you wish to pray for somebody whose name is Anjali, then you would say:

oṁ tāre tuttāre ture svāḥ
Anjali Ayuḥ punya Jñānā puṣtiṃ kuru svā

Shloka 3 for healing wounds

oṁ namo bhagavate
mahā sudarśanā
vasudevā dhanvantārāyā
amṛtā kalasā hasthāyā
sarva bhaya vināsāyā
sarva rogā nivārānāyā
thrī lokya paṭhāye
thrī lokya nithāye
śrī mahā viṣṇu svarūpā
śrī dhanvantarī svarūpā
śrī śrī śrī
ouṣatā cakrā nārāyaṇā svāḥ

Meaning

We pray to the God who is known as Sudarshana Vasudev Dhanvantari
Who holds the pot full of the nectar of immortality.
Destroyer of all fears,

Destroyer of all diseases
Preserver of the three worlds like Lord Vishnu who is empowered to heal the jiva souls.
We bow to you.

Devotional songs

In Hindu mythology, Goddess Durga, a powerful form of Parvati, is thought of as the destroyer of all evil. The Durga Sapta Slokhi shloka talks about the different attributes of the Goddess. After chanting this shloka several times you will realise that each one of us is blessed with the divine strength that is required to face physical pain, and this shloka infuses you with that strength. Listen to the Durga Pancharatnam stotram sung by M.S. Subbulakshmi. She sings the shloka at an easily understandable pace.

Restorative yoga asanas

Note: Yoga after surgery must be done with utmost care. Please consult with your surgeon before you start doing any exercises.

Restorative yoga is very helpful in allowing the body to slowly move back to normalcy. Using props such as cushions and blocks help to perform these asanas with ease. A simple search on the Internet will help to get a visual understanding of the asana.

The following asanas help to heal the body and restore it to its normal state:

- Balasana
- Savasana
- Viparita karani (Perform with a cushion against your back and legs on the wall)
- Adho mukha svanasana

- Supta virasana (Perform with a prop like a cushion to protect your back)
- Supta baddha konasana (This can be done even while lying down on the bed)

Temples to visit

The Ashta Dasa Bhuja Mahalakshmi Durga temple, situated in Kurichi, Puddukottai, is thought to have the power to heal any physical wound. The deity is made of navapashanam (nine herbal ingredients) and has eighteen hands. Legend has it that a man named Dhanaramlinga Thevar used to heal and give medicines to the poor in Kuruchi and the surrounding areas. He was once asked to perform the consecration of a Durga temple. At the same time, the Goddess appeared in front of him and told him to imagine the way he would like the idol to be. The Goddess said the idol would be created by a siddhar (a person who treats people with naturopathic medicines) in accordance with Dhanaramalinga Thevar's requirements. The siddhar arrived and created this beautiful idol with eighteen hands, sitting on a lion, made of navapashanam.

The Shri Danvantri Arogya Peedam situated in Walajapet, twenty kilometres east of Vellore in Tamil Nadu, is known for its restorative powers.

Heal Your Eyes

> 'Yoga does not just change the way we see things, it transforms the person who sees.'
>
> – *B.K.S. Iyengar*

Good eye care consists of good nutrition and regular check-ups with an ophthalmologist. If you are recovering from eye surgery, your ophthalmologist would have walked you through the dos and don'ts, but given here are some general tips:

- Wash your hands regularly as this is really the first line of defence against any infection.
- Do not touch the tips of the eyedrop bottle.
- Use an eye mask to calm your eyes. This forces you to close your eyes and get much-needed rest as well.
- Do not lift weights after eye surgery. This exerts pressure on the eyes and should be avoided. Lifting babies is also not advisable after eye surgery.
- Do not use eye makeup such as kajal. This can increase the chances of an eye infection.

- Wear sunglasses that have UV protection. This will protect you from the harsh sun's rays.
- Ask your doctor for the warning signs of a change in vision that you need to look out for.

With the increased use of computers and gadgets, eyes are under a lot more stress now, which means they also require a lot more rest. The tips below will help you become more aware of your eyes and take care of them:

- ***Choose an easy-to-read font***: While technology can be fun, the choice of font could make a significant difference to your experience with it. If you are experiencing low vision, choose fonts that make reading easier, such as Verdana, Arial or Helvetica. These fonts come with a fixed width and are called sans serif, which means they do not have the small projections at the end of the letters, making them easier to read.
- ***Use the zoom level***: You don't have to zoom in so much that you have to scroll to read the next word, just make the page big enough that you aren't squinting when reading something.
- ***Use the 10-10-10 rule***: You have probably heard about the 10-10-10 rule in making decisions. Ophthalmologists recommend the 10-10-10 rule in eye care — every ten minutes look at something about ten feet away, for ten seconds. It gives your eyes a much-needed break.
- ***Use bright light***: Correct lighting is essential while using the computer. Do not read or use the computer in darkness, especially while lying in bed, as it could really hurt your eyes.

- ***Keep your distance***: Ensure that the distance you keep from your computer or gadget is adequate. The recommended distance is 1.5 to 2 feet. Ensure that you look at the computer screen straight and are not looking down at it.

Choose from the foods below to ensure that you have a diet rich in the required nutrients to keep your eyes naturally healthy:

- Foods rich in vitamin A, such as carrot, yellow squash, sweet potato, mango, spinach and cantaloupe help in preventing macular-related diseases and even dryness of the eyes. Zinc helps the body to absorb vitamin A and can be found in wheat and nuts.
- Vitamin C, a powerful antioxidant, is good for retinal health and is found abundantly in foods such as citrus fruits, berries, red and yellow pepper, tropical fruits, potatoes and green leafy vegetables.
- Lutein acts as good protection and helps in maintaining retinal health. Green leafy vegetables such as spinach and kale are good sources of lutein as long as the water in which they are boiled or cooked is not thrown away. Yellow and orange fruits and vegetables, such as corn and yellow squash, are good sources too.
- Omega 3 fatty acids are known to prevent dry eyes. The best source of omega 3 fatty acids is fish. If you are a vegetarian, consult with your ophthalmologist if you can take omega 3, 6 or 9 supplements.
- Refrain from alcohol and quit smoking.

Shloka for the eyes

Chant the following while performing the Surya Namaskar. Chant one line with each change of posture.

1. Start with pranamasana, breathe normally and chant, '*oṁ mitrāya namaḥ*'
2. Inhale and go into hastauttanaasana while chanting, '*oṁ ravaye namaḥ*'
3. Exhale and perform the hastapadanasana while chanting, '*oṁ sūryāya namaḥ*'
4. Inhale and go into the ashwa sanchalanasana while chanting, '*oṁ bhānave namaḥ*'
5. Exhale and perform the adho mukha svanasana while chanting, '*oṁ khagāya namaḥ*'
6. Inhale and go into the ashtanga namaskar and chant, '*oṁ pūṣṇe namaḥ*'
7. Exhale and perform bhujangasana and chant, '*oṁ hiraṇyagarbhāya namaḥ*'
8. Inhale and perform adho mukha svanasana again, while chanting, '*oṁ marīcaye namaḥ*'
9. Exhale and perform the ashwa sanchalanasana, while chanting, '*oṁ ādityāya namaḥ*'
10. Inhale and perform the hastapadnasana while chanting, '*oṁ savitre namaḥ*'
11. Exhale and perform the hastauttanaasana while chanting, '*oṁ arkāya namaḥ*'
12. Conclude with pranamasana, breathe normally and chant '*oṁ bhāskarāya namaḥ*'

Repeat the twelve poses in quick succession as in Vinyasa yoga. There should be a smooth flow from one pose to the next for optimum benefits.

Meaning

Salutations to the One Who is Affectionate to All
Salutations to the One Who is the Cause for Change
Salutations to the One Who Induces Activity
Salutations to the One Who Diffuses Light
Salutations to the One Who Moves in the Sky
Salutations to the One Who Nourishes All
Salutations to the One Who Contains Everything
Salutations to the One Who Possesses Rays
Salutations to the One Who is God of Gods
Salutations to the One Who Produces Everything
Salutations to the One Who is Fit to Be Worshipped
Salutations to the One Who is the Cause of Lustre

Devotional songs

The Aditya Hridayam is a hymn singing the praise of the Sun God and was recited by the great sage Agastya to boost Shri Rama's morale before the war. It takes about nine minutes to chant along with the great singer, M.S. Subbulakshmi.

Yoga asanas for eye problems

The surya namaskar is one of the most effective asanas to perform to help heal your eyes quicker. Preferably perform the asana in an area that gets sunlight, but protect your eyes well from direct rays.

Temples to visit

The Kannudayanayaki Amman (meaning Goddess who 'gives' eyes) temple in Nattarasankottai, Tamil Nadu is very famous.

The mythology behind this temple is as follows.

Some buttermilk merchants from Nataarasan Kottai were travelling to a nearby village to sell their wares, but were hit by some power at a particular place, causing them to lose all their buttermilk. Scared and confused, they decided to take the matter to the king. The night before they approached him for help, the king had a dream in which the Goddess appeared, explaining that the reason the merchants could not go past that particular place was because her idol was buried there. She instructed the king to unearth the idol.

While the king's workers were trying to dig up the idol, one of the men swung his spade too high and it hit his own eye, causing it to bleed. He continued to dig for the idol. Once the statue was unearthed and was taken out, his eye was miraculously healed.

The presiding deity is fondly known as Kannathal, meaning Mother (Protector) of eyes.

Other temples famous for helping devotees with eye problems include the Velleeswarar temple in Chennai and the Kannayiram Udayar temple, in Kurumanakudi, Tamil Nadu.

Heal Your Back

'Every human being is the author of his own health or disease. Disease is the result of disobedience to the immutable laws of health that govern life.'

– *Swami Sivananda*

Back-related problems are fast increasing in today's world because of the long hours that people spend sitting in front of computers with bad posture. Back problems tend to creep up on you slowly and they're quite difficult to get rid of. The spinal cord connects the body to the brain through an extensive system of nerves. Any disruption to this very delicate system results in the entire human body going completely out of whack. Following the tips given here can provide some basic care for spine health:

- ***Weigh the pros and cons***: Carrying or lifting heavy objects puts a lot of pressure on the back. Do not lift weights if you are pregnant. If you have no choice but to lift a weight, bend your knees before you do so. This lessens the pressure on the back. Lift weights, including babies, only if you really have to.

- ***Don't throw your weight around***: Wearing the right footwear is imperative to correct body posture and hence for good spinal health. Long hours of working and walking on very high heels is bound to put pressure on your back and legs. Get appropriate footwear that suits your lifestyle and work.
- ***Don't get weighed down***: The pressure to continue doing your normal chores even after surgery or an injury to the back would always be there, especially if you are very independent-minded. Don't get weighed down by the pressure you put on yourself. Give yourself a break and delegate work to others at home.
- ***Watch your weight***: Obesity is often a leading cause of back problems. Ensure that you exercise regularly to keep your body weight in check. Pregnant women suffer from back-related problems during and after pregnancy because of the added weight of the baby. Correct pre- and post-natal exercises will help ensure that the spine health is well-preserved.

Controlling and managing pain is key in getting your back to heal quickly. A balanced diet will also help maintain a good body weight. The following Indian foods are known to lessen pain:

- Nuts and oilseeds in the form of pine nuts, pumpkin seeds, almonds, walnuts, etc. are an excellent source of zinc and phosphorous. These minerals will help to ensure that antioxidants, which help control pain, are provided to the body in good measure.
- Green leafy vegetables and yellow fruits and vegetables not only provide fibre but also the required folic acid requirements of the body. They

also provide vitamin K, which is required for calcium absorption in the body.

- Calcium and vitamin D are required for bone-building and maintenance of bones. Moderate consumption of dairy products such as yoghurt, milk and cheese helps to ensure that the required doses of calcium are addressed. Ensure you exercise outside to get your daily dose of natural vitamin D from the sun. In case you are not able to get out in the sun much, check with your doctor to ensure your vitamin D levels are within normal limits. Dark chocolates are an incredibly rich source of magnesium and so are almonds, cashews and sunflower seeds. This mineral is required in bone-building and maintenance processes.

Shloka for the back

The following powerful mantra is chanted to heal and rectify health problems connected with the spine and limbs. Chant it while performing the yoga asanas suggested below.

oṁ vakratundāya ḥum

Meaning

Vakratundaya refers to Lord Ganesha's trunk; by saying 'hum', we seek His immediate intervention in resolving our suffering.

Yoga asanas for the back

The following poses strengthen the spine and help back-related issues.

- Garudasana
- Balasana

- Ardha padmasana or Siddhasana.
- Utkatasana

Devotional songs

'Kurai Onrum Illai' (meaning 'I do not have any problems') is a Tamil devotional song written by C. Rajagopalachari. Listen to the version sung by M.S. Subbulakshmi. This song makes you feel gratitude for all that you have. The Ganesha shloka Vakratunda Mahakaya, as sung by Shankar Mahadevan, is a very upbeat song that is sure to help you forget your pain.

Temples to visit

If you visit any temple in India and observe the devotees, you will find that they go around the temple structure in a clockwise direction three or five times. Usually the temples are large and just walking around the structure and chanting gets the body to move and stretches the lower back and spine.

The Bhoominathar temple in Puddukkottai, Tamil Nadu, is known to help cure problems with the back and hip. Devotees also go to this temple when they fear earthquakes or require settlements in land disputes.

Legend has it that Bhooma Devi (Mother Earth) had to do penance in order to be able to sustain the growing population of the world over many billions of years. Lord Shiva appeared before her and told her that her penance was sufficient, but her devotees would need to continue to pray on her behalf in Kali Yuga (the current period of mankind). Lord Bhoominathar was one of the Lords she prayed to.

Heal Your Stomach

> 'Those who eat too much or eat too little, who sleep too much or sleep too little, will not succeed in meditation. But those who are temperate in eating and sleeping, work and recreation, will come to the end of sorrow through meditation.'
>
> – *Bhagavad Gita*

If you are recovering from abdominal surgery or abdominal pain, and are resting on your back, ensure that you follow these tips to ensure your stomach is well-protected:

- Change your position slowly so the effort does not overexert your stomach. Place your hand on one side and turn, so that the weight of your body is not felt on your stomach.
- Exercise your ankles frequently, so they don't cramp.
- Take care while coughing or while taking deep breaths. It can cause a lot of pressure on sutures, if any, on the abdomen.
- Go for short walks; use a crutch if required.

Stress and the stomach

Most of us think of stress as something that only affects our brain. However, the first organ to get affected by stress is often the stomach. Stress both causes and comes from a bad diet, long hours between meals, unhealthy dietary practices, over-indulgence and a host of other food-related issues that trigger hyperacidity and stomach-related problems. Stress tends to magnify the negative effects of all bad habits.

- One of the best ways to decrease the workload on the stomach is to ensure that the type of foods eaten or the frequency with which they are eaten are controlled and monitored. If you are recovering from digestive issues, then follow the rules below to help to bring the digestion back on track (as always, please consult with your dietitian before implementing them): Listen to your body's needs. The body inherently knows what to avoid, especially when sick. Tune in to your body's needs and that is the best way to heal faster. Remember the first sign of inability to digest food comes from just the smell. If your nose tells you that you can't handle it and you will feel sick if you eat it — then believe your nose!
- First start by avoiding habits and food products that burden digestion, such as alcohol, smoking and processed, oily and fatty foods.
- Next heal your stomach slowly by eating small meals frequently. Drink eight to ten glasses of water every day to ensure your body does not go into a dehydrated state. Take added vitamin and mineral supplements to help heal the stomach quicker, after consulting with your physician.

- Slowly introduce foods that are rich in probiotic bacteria (also known as good bacteria). This is essential for digestion. This is found abundantly in home-made yoghurts or store-bought yoghurt that specifically mentions 'probiotic-added' on the cover. Along with this, consume foods that are unprocessed and easily digestible, like clear soup (without any spices), rice, red and green gram lentils, dals and soft boiled vegetables. Use minimal oil.
- Finally, introduce other foods slowly into your diet. Increase the spice and oil levels in accordance with your condition. Stay away from meat products and oily foods till you are able to digest normal foods without a problem.

Shloka for the stomach

When one is in pain or discomfort, it would be highly impossible to chant a shloka that is difficult to memorise; therefore, choose any shloka that you know well and that helps you calm your mind.

The following shloka from Chapter 15 of the *Bhagavad Gita* can be chanted after ingesting food. This will aid digestion.

ahaṁ vaiśvānaro bhūtvāṁ prāṇināṁ dehamāśritaḥ
prāṇāpānasamāyukta: pacāmyannaṁ caturvidhama

Meaning

'I am the fire of digestion in the bodies of all living entities, and I join with the air of life, outgoing and incoming, to digest the four kinds of foodstuff, such as food that is swallowed, food that is chewed, food that is licked, and food that is sucked.

Yoga asanas to aid digestion

Learn these asanas from a good yoga teacher and include them in a fifteen-minute daily routine.

- Apnasana, which will help relieve gas in the stomach.
- Natrajasana, which helps soothe the stomach and tone the abdominal muscles.
- Sethu bandasana, which helps blood flow through the body, thus aiding digestion.
- Ardha matsyendrasana, which relieves bloating.

Devotional songs

The Soundarya Lahari, literally meaning 'waves of beauty', was written by Shri Adi Shankaracharya in praise of Goddess Parvati's beauty. This ancient Sanskrit text is known to have miraculous healing properties for many ailments of the human body. It is a collection of hundred shlokas and the version sung by T.S. Ranganathan takes about an hour to listen to. The entire song is split into sets of ten. Shloka 41 is the one that helps heal the stomach.

Temples to visit

The Thiruvadhigai Veerattaneswarar temple in Panruti, Tamil Nadu, is dedicated to Lord Shiva. The presiding deity, Shri Veerattaneswarar, is known to have miraculous healing powers for the stomach.

The mythological story behind this temple is that the saint Tirunavukkarasar, although born to a family who believed in the worship of Lord Shiva, decided to adopt Jainism in his younger years and left home to embrace that religion. His sister Thilagavathy, a staunch devotee of Lord Shiva, prayed very hard for his return. Once, Tirunavukkarasar suffered from intense and unbearable stomach ache. His sister requested him to come back and took him to the Thiruvadhigai Veerattaneswarar temple, applied the sacred ash on his forehead, and is said to have chanted the shloka *oṁ ṇama śivāya* with complete devotion. Tirunavukkarasar's stomach pain is said to have disappeared almost instantaneously. He was so taken in by this miracle that he immediately started worshipping Lord Shiva and proceeded to write many hymns in praise of the Lord that are very popular till date.

Other temples famous for helping devotees with stomach problems include the Sandhana Mariamman temple in Madurai and the Lakshmi Narayana Temple in Thanjavur.

Heal Your Reproductive Organs

'To be born at all is a miracle'

– *The Dalai Lama*

Procreation is arguably the most natural aspect of human life. The human body is an extremely fine-tuned bio-alarm. Puberty usually occurs between ten to thirteen years of age for girls, signified by their first period, and around twelve for boys, with the development of primary sex organs. The body continues to develop during the teenage years. Doctors feel the ideal age for a woman to have a baby is around twenty-one to thirty, and menopause sets in around fifty. Of course, this is different from woman to woman. However, for reasons we don't understand yet, stress, unhealthy food habits, irregular sleeping patterns and lack of exercise disrupt these natural cycles and lead to various other conditions.

Like all organs of the body, special care is also required for the reproductive organs. Some tips given here are applicable to both male and female reproductive organs:

- ***Shower every day***: Our ancestors knew it all! The only way they could ensure that people maintained a standard of hygiene was to introduce a religious element to it. That is why they insisted on having a bath before prayers. Keeping the body clean is imperative to good health. Washing the private parts of the body with a good soap keeps any form of infection away.
- ***Wear comfortable clothing***: The pressure to look good and slim has always been there, but it seems to be increasingly gaining importance. Ensure that the undergarments that you wear are not tight-fitting. It is important that there is good air circulation and that the organs are not compressed.
- ***Perform self-examinations regularly***: Testicular self-examinations or breast self-examinations are very important on a regular basis after puberty. This needs to be done correctly and it is best done with the help of the doctor initially. If you are shy about touching your own body, consult a physician or gynaecologist who would help you overcome this shyness and teach you the correct way to look for unusual signs of growth on these organs.
- ***Protect yourself while playing sports***: Contact sports can sometimes cause harm to the reproductive organs because of the impact from a fast-moving object such as a cricket ball. Ensure that you are well-protected while playing such sports.

- ***Practise safe sex***: First, this is not a taboo topic anymore. It is imperative to spell things out clearly, as prevention is always better than cure. While premarital sex is not being promoted here, it is important to recognise that it is being practised increasingly, even in conservative societies of the world. Ensure that you are honest with your doctor and understand what it is to practise safe sex.
- ***Treat infections immediately***: Do not be laidback in attending to any type of infection affecting your reproductive organs. Get professional medical help and attend to it immediately.
- ***Do not push your biological clock***: There is a time and place for everything, including having babies. The biological clock starts ticking for men and women by the time they are thirty. Recognise that it is not just about having the baby, but also about caring for this beautiful bundle of joy for the rest of his / her life. Prepare to have a baby as soon as you are ready for it, but do not wait for *all* the stars to align. There never is the 'perfect' time.

A cardinal rule for a well-functioning reproductive system, be it a man or a woman, is a good balanced diet. Follow these general rules to ensure your reproductive organs remain healthy and you are able to conceive normally:

- ***Follow a balanced diet***: Consult with your nutritionist and determine if calories need to be increased and when. The calories should come from healthy carbohydrate and protein sources and not as empty calories from foods such as carbonated drinks and high-calorie foods.

- ***Eat small meals frequently***: This is a key factor to prevent heartburn and other complications such as vitamin and mineral deficiencies during pregnancy.
- ***Avoid excessive consumption of caffeine and alcohol***: Both of these tend to dehydrate the system and prevent the absorption of important minerals in the body.
- ***Increase the intake of water per day***: A well-hydrated body ensures that the food moves along in the body well, minerals and vitamins are absorbed well and that toxins are eliminated. If you have water retention, then ensure that you consult with a doctor before increasing water intake. Cut back on excessive salt intake. This will help in decreasing water retention in the body.
- ***Avoid processed foods***: Stay away from refined carbohydrates such as refined wheat flour. Essential vitamins and fibre are lost in the process while preparing refined carbohydrates.
- ***Protein up***: Energise your body with high-quality proteins. Foods rich in proteins such as legumes also tend to produce flatulence, so do try and have yoghurt-based foods while increasing the legumes in your diet.
- ***Avoid soya-rich foods***: There is documented evidence now that soya-rich foods hinder fertility. It is best to avoid or consume in extreme moderation soya-rich foods such as vegetable burgers and soya milk. If you are lactose-intolerant and have been using soya milk, switch to almond milk instead.

Shloka for uterine health

oṁ Garbharakakṣāṁbikāẏai ca vidmahe
mangala devatāyai ca dhīmahi
tannau devī pracotayāt

Meaning

Om, let us meditate on Garbarakshambikaayai
The auspicious angel
And let Goddess Devi illuminate our mind

Devotional dongs

The Garbarakshambigai Kavacham, sung by Sudha Raghunathan in praise of the Mother Goddess takes less than ten minutes to listen to, and is very pleasing to the ears.

Yoga asanas to boost fertility

The following asanas are known to help improve fertility. These asanas can be performed along with medical treatment.
Note: Learn the following yoga postures from an experienced yoga instructor. Performing these yoga asanas in an incorrect fashion will cause more physical problems.

- Paschimottanasana
- Hastapadasana
- Badhakonasana
- Viparita Karani

Temples to visit

It is believed that visiting the Garbarakshambigai temple in Thanjavur helps cure infertility-related problems in women, and also helps them have a safe and trouble-free delivery. Legend has it that when Vedhikai, an ardent devotee of Goddess Garbarakshambigai, almost lost her foetus, the Goddess came to the rescue and blessed her by saving her baby and giving her a baby boy. It is believed that the compassionate Goddess fulfils every parent's dream to have a healthy child.

Another temple to visit, where the Goddess is believed to help infertility-related problems, is the Karuvalarcheri temple in Kumbakonam.

Shloka to heal infertility in men

This Gopala Gayatri Mantra can be chanted by both men and women to heal infertility. Women can chant this shloka for men who have infertility issues.

oṁ gopālāya vidmahe gopījanavallabhāya dhīmahi
tanno gopāla: pracodayāta

Meaning

Om, let us meditate on Gopala,
Let us meditate on the dear friend of the gopikas,
May Lord Gopala illuminate our mind.

Devotional songs

The Putra Prapti Astakam written by Shri Mukkur Lakshmi Narasimhachariyar is known to be very effective in overcoming difficulties in bearing children. This shloka is in praise of Lord Narasimha in Mattapalli, Andhra Pradesh.

Yoga asanas for improving fertility in men

The following asanas are known to help improve fertility. They can be performed along with medical treatment.

- Viparita karani
- Mahamudra
- Hastapadasana

Temples to visit

The Shri Santhana Venugopala Swamy temple (Huchappa Gopala) at Hemmaragala Grama, Nanjangud taluk, Mysore, is known to bless couples with children. Legend has it that a Chola king wanted a boy after having twelve girls so he prayed to the presiding deity there, Gopala. The king and queen spent the night there with their baby who they had wished was a boy. The next morning, they saw that the baby girl had become a boy. The Chola king then named the deity 'Huchappa' Gopala, or Crazy Gopala, after this miracle occurred.

The Shri Puthrakameshtiswarar temple in Tiruvannamalai district, Tamil Nadu, is also known to bless couples with children.

Wholesomeness and Bliss

> 'It is like a lighted torch whose flame can be distributed to ever so many other torches which people may bring along; and therewith they will cook food and dispel darkness, while the original torch itself remains burning ever the same. It is even so with the bliss of the Way.'
>
> – *Gautama Buddha*

What next?

This journey that we call life takes us through different types of challenges. Sometimes we have the mental and physical energy to deal with these challenges and sometimes we do not. But all these challenges, if analysed after the unsettling time has passed, have an embedded lesson in them. The lesson may be about controlling hunger, speaking up for yourself, being more careful about money, and so on…

These are lessons to reshape ourselves. To adapt. To change. To grow. To evolve.

According to the Dalai Lama, 'It is ... very helpful to think of adversity not so much as a threat to our peace of mind but rather as the very means by which patience is attained.' At every important milestone in our lives, we must allow ourselves to be connected closer to a wholesome state — a state where the desire to be recognised or appreciated is lessened, a state where the desire to possess material things is lowered, and a state where you start to love the inner you, bringing you closer to the higher power.

The wholesome state that we transform ourselves into can give nothing but bliss.

Quoting the very famous Gayatri mantra, I invoke the blessings of the Almighty to grant us this bliss in our never-ending pursuit of happiness:

oṁ bhūrbhuvaḥ suvaḥ
tatsaviturvareṇyaṁ
bhargo devasya dhīmahi
dhiyo yo naḥ pracodayāt

An approximate translation of the above would be:

Om, that Divine Illumination which pervades the Universe,
That Divine Illumination which is the most adorable,
On that Divine Radiance we meditate,
May that enlighten our intellect and awaken our spiritual wisdom.

Lighting one more lamp as a mark of completion for this edition of the book, please read the following insightful verse from the *Isha Upanishad*:

oṁ pūrṇamadaḥ pūrṇamidaṁ pūrṇātpurṇamudacyate
pūrṇaśya pūrṇamādāya pūrṇamevāvaśiṣyate
oṁ śāntiḥ śāntiḥ śāntiḥ

One form of translation to the above verse would be:
Om, completeness is that, completeness is this, from completeness, completeness comes forth.
Completeness from completeness taken away,
Completeness to completeness added,
Completeness alone remains.
Om, peace (in me), peace (in nature), peace (in divine forces)

Shlokas in This Book

The table below provides, as a quick reference, all the shlokas used in this book.

Shlokas to Overcome Obstacles

oṁ gam ganapataye namaḥ
vakratuṇḍa mahākāya sūryakoṭi samaprabha nirvighnam kuru me deva sarva kāryeśusarvadā
gajānanaṁ bhūtagaṇādi sevitaṁ kapittha jambūphalasāra bhakṣitam umāsutaṁ śoka vināśakāraṇaṁ namāmi vighneśvara pādapaṅkajam
Ganesha Pancharathnam

Shlokas for Peace

oṁ sumukhāya namaḥ
om śāntimatyai namaḥ
oṁ saha nāvavatu saha nau bhunaktu saha vīryaṁ karavāvahai tejasvi_nāvadhītamastu mā vidviṣāvahai oṁ śāntiḥ śāntiḥ śāntiḥ

oṁ mani padme hūṁ
Kaamaakshi Stotram

Shlokas to Find Something that is Lost

oṁ araikāsu ammane potri
karāgre vasate lakṣmiḥ karamadhye sarasvati karamūle tu govindaḥ prabhāte karadarśanam
Lalitha Ashtothram

Shlokas to Overcome Anxiety

buddhir balam yaśo dhairyam nirbhayatvam arogatām ajāḍyam vāk paṭutvam ca hanumat smaraṇāt bhavet
Hanuman Chalisa

Shlokas to Overcome Fear of Spouse's Wellbeing

kātyāyani mahāmāye mahāyoginyadhīśvari nanda gopasutaṁ devipatiṁ me kuru te namaḥ
patnīṁ manoramāṁ dehi manovṛtānu sāriṇīm tāriṇīm durga saṁsāra sāgarasya kulodbhavāma
Durga Pancharatnam

Shlokas to Heal Marital Discord

sarvamaṅgalamāṅgalye śive sarvārthasādhike śaraṇye tryambake gauri nārāyaṇi namo'stu te
Om Jaya Jaya Jaya Shakthi
Ardha Nareeswara Stotram

Shlokas for Better Relationships

oṁ ṣrīm mahālakṣmīyai namaḥ
Mahalakshmi Ashtakam

Shlokas to Remember Your Beginnings and Cherish Family

mātṛu devo bhava, pitṛu devo bhava, ācārya devo bhava, athithi devo bhava
Pandava Gita Verse 28 tvameva mātā ca pitā tvameva tvameva bandhuśca sakhā tvameva tvameva vidyā draviṇam tvameva tvameva sarvam mama deva deva

Shlokas to Overcome Guilt

oṁ harāya namaḥ
Shiva Aparadha Kshamapana Stotram

Shlokas for Abundance and Prosperity

oṁ śrī mahālakṣmyai ca vidmahe viṣṇu patnyai ca dhīmahi tanno lakṣmī pracodayāt
Kanakadhara Stotram or Sri Suktham

Shlokas to Heal Oneself from Emotional Problems

oṁ āpadām apahartāram dātāram sarvasaṁpadām lokābhirāmam śrīrāmam bhūyo bhūyo namāmyaham
vanamālī gadī ṣār'ngī ṣa'nkhī cakrī ca nandakī ṣrīmān nārāyaṇo vishṇuh vāsudevo'bhirakshatu
Vishnu Sahasranāmam

Shlokas for Nourishment

annapūrṇe sadāpūrṇe shaṇkara-prāṇavallabhe jnāna-vairāgya siddhyarthaṁ bhikṣhāṁ dehi cha Parvati
Annapoorna Ashtakam

Shlokas to Gain Knowledge

sarasvati namastubhyaṁ varade kāmarūpiṇi vidyārambhaṁ kariṣyāmi siddhirbhavatu me sadā
gururbrahmā gururviṣṇurgururdevo maheśvaraḥ gurureva paraṁ brahma taṣmai śrīgurave namaḥ
Dakshinamurthy Stotram

Shlokas for Freedom of Ignorance and to Seek Wisdom

oṁ asato mā sadgamaya tamaso mā jyotirgamaya mṛtyormā amṛtaṁ gamaya oṁ śāntiḥ śāntiḥ śāntiḥ
Bhaja Govindam

Shlokas to Excel in Education

jñānānanda mayaṁ devaṁ nirmalam sphaṭikākṛtiṁ ādhāraṁ sarvavidyānaṁ hayagrīvaṁ upāsmahe
Saraswati Vandana Shloka

Shlokas to Build Self-Confidence

manojavaṁ mārutatulyavegaṁ jitendriyaṁ buddhimatāṁ variṣṭhaṁ vātātmajaṁ vānarayūthamukhyaṁ śrīrāmadūtaṁ śaraṇaṁ prapadye
Hanuman Ashtothram

Shlokas to Ward off the Evil Eye

ŏm āparajeethaya Vidmahe Pratyangiraya ḍheemahi ṭhano ūgra pracodhayāth… ŏm Pratayangiraya Vidmahe ṣathrunisoothiniya ḍheemahi ṭhano ḍevi Prajothayāth

Mahishasuramardhini Stotram or Kandhar Sashti Kavacham

Shlokas for the Golden Years of Life

oṁ īśā vāsyamidaṁ sarvaṁ yatkiñca jagatyāṁ jagat
tena tyaktena bhuñjīthā mā gṛdhaḥ kasyasviddhanam

Namo ratna trayāya Shloka

Shlokas to Heal the Body of Physical Problems

oṁ tryambakaṁ yajāmahe
sugandhiṁ puṣṭivardhanam
urvārukamiva bandhanān
mṛtyormukṣīya māmṛtāt

Dhanavantri Maha Mantra Japam

Shlokas to Heal Wounds

aham ārogyaṁ

oṁ tāre tuttāre ture svāḥ
mama Ayuḥ punya Jñānā puṣtiṃ kuru svāh

oṁ namo bhagavate
mahā sudarśanā
vasudevā dhanvantārāyā
amṛtā kalasā hasthāyā
sarva bhaya vināsāyā
sarva rogā nivārānāyā
thrī lokya paṭhāye
thrī lokya nithāye
śrī mahā viṣṇu svarūpā
śrī dhanvantarī svarūpā
śrī śrī śrī
ouṣatā cakrā nārāyaṇā svāḥ

Durga Sapta Slokhi Shlokas

Shlokas to Heal the Eyes

oṁ mitrāya namaḥ oṁ ravaye namaḥ oṁ sūryāya namaḥ oṁ bhānave namaḥ oṁ khagāya namaḥ oṁ pūṣṇe namaḥ oṁ hiraṇyagarbhāya namaḥ oṁ marīcaye namaḥ oṁ ādityāya namaḥ oṁ savitre namaḥ oṁ arkāya namaḥ oṁ bhāskarāya namaḥ
Aditya Hridayam

Shlokas to Heal the Back

oṁ vakratundāya ḥum
Kurai Ondum Illai

Shlokas to Heal Stomach

ahaṁ vaiśvānaro bhūtvāṁ prāṇināṁ dehamāśritaḥ prāṇāpānasamāyukta: pacāmyannaṁ caturvidhama
Soundarya Lahari

Shlokas to Heal Female Reproductive Organs

oṁ Garbharakakṣāṁbikāẏai ca vidmahe mangala devatāyai ca dhīmahi tannau devī pracotayāt
Garbarakshambigai Kavacham

Shlokas to Heal Male Reproductive Organs

oṁ gopālāya vidmahe gopījanavallabhāya dhīmahi tanno gopāla: pracodayāta

Puthra Prapthi Ashtakam

Shlokas for Wholesomeness and Bliss

oṁ bhūrbhuvaḥ suvaḥ tatsaviturvareṇyaṁ bhargo devasya dhīmahi dhiyo yo naḥ pracodayāt
oṁ pūrṇamadaḥ pūrṇamidaṁ pūrṇātpurṇamudacyate pūrṇaśya pūrṇamādāya pūrṇamevāvaśiṣyate oṁ śāntiḥ śāntiḥ śāntiḥ